Mrs Beeton's
Christmas Menus

MRS BEETON'S
Christmas Menus

Creative ideas for festive entertaining

Consultant Editor
BRIDGET JONES

WARD LOCK

Contents

Menus for Sharing and Celebrating

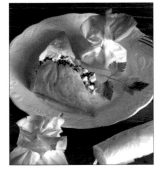

Planning Perfect Menus

Enjoying good food in the company of friends is one of life's greatest pleasures, and when the host and hostess are relaxed and everything has been well planned, the occasion is certain to be a success.

The key points to consider when planning a menu, apart from the likes and dislikes or dietary restrictions of the diners, are the flavours, textures, colour and weight of the meal. A well-planned menu balances all these elements. Practical aspects to consider are your ability and confidence as a cook; the budget and the cooking facilities available.

When planning a menu, it is usual to consider the main course of the meal first, then to fit the starter, fish course or dessert around it. This does not always have to be the rule – if you have a particularly splendid starter or dessert which you want to serve at a dinner party, or even for a family get-together, there is absolutely no reason why you should not use it as the focus of the meal. If, for example, you wanted to serve a chocolate fondue as the finale of a dinner party, it would be logical to keep the preceding courses light. Equally, traditional steamed sponge pudding with custard is a real family treat but is not suitable for serving after a very filling main course, so a light salad and grilled fish would be the better option.

FLAVOURS AND TEXTURES

As well as considering the accompaniments for the main dish, remember that a strongly flavoured starter will put a lightly seasoned main course in the shade, just as a very spicy main course will ruin the palate for a delicate dessert. Balance strong flavours and aim to accentuate more subtle dishes.

Texture is a less obvious but equally important characteristic of food. A meal that consists solely of soft food is dull, and three courses of dry or crunchy dishes can be a disaster, leaving everyone gasping for water. Balance soft and smooth mixtures with crunchy textures; combine moist dishes with dry ones. Offer crisp salads with zesty dressings to counteract rich fried foods; serve plain, crunchy, lightly cooked vegetables to balance heavily sauced casseroles and stews.

COLOUR AND WEIGHT

Recognising the importance of colour in a dish and on a menu is not merely a matter of dropping a piece of parsley on to a grey sauce. The ingredients used in individual dishes, the quality of cooking juices and sauces and the choice of accompaniments are all factors in achieving a menu that looks as good as it tastes. Some cooked foods inevitably look un-interesting; this is when the choice of accompaniments is vital. Flavour and texture must also be considered.

The overall weight of the meal is important. Light dishes should balance richer foods. A filling dish should always be flanked by delicate courses.

FOOD VALUE AND SPECIAL DIETS

Dinner parties and special meals are occasions for breaking or bending the rules and indulging in favourite foods.

Special diets are a different matter, so always check if any guests have particular dietary restrictions for social or medical reasons. Plan these into the menu for all diners as far as possible. In some cases, for example when catering for vegetarians as well as meat eaters, it is quite possible to provide one menu to suit everyone. Contemporary vegetarian dishes are acceptable to all, not simply to those who avoid animal products; it is far trickier to plan a vegan menu to suit all tastes. Limitations imposed for health reasons may be more difficult to accommodate; if in doubt, ask the prospective guest or consult an official source of information for guidance.

If the whole menu cannot be adapted to suit everyone, plan the meal around one or two of the key

dishes. It is usually quite easy to choose a first course that will suit all diets. Either the main dish or vegetable accompaniments should be selected for their versatility: if the main dish is unsuitable for certain diners, then the vegetable accompaniments should make equally interesting main dishes on their own. For example, ratatouille, a mixed vegetable gratin or stir-fried vegetables with noodles are all suitable for serving with plain meat dishes, but make an equally good vegetarian meal when served with the right accompaniments.

PARTIES

The choice of party food depends on the number of guests and the budget – these factors influence the style of food, choice of ingredients, balance of hot and cold dishes and the number of courses. Whether you are planning a formal meal or cocktail-style buffet with snacks and nibbles, remember the following points as they are crucial to the success – or failure – of the chosen menu.

- Time available for food preparation.
- Refrigerator space for storing ingredients and/or dishes which require chilling.
- Kitchen facilities, particularly oven and hob space.
- Freezer space and suitability of dishes for preparing in advance.
- Availability of crockery and cutlery for serving.
- The time available for last-minute work, finishing dishes, garnishing and so on.
- Your own ability as cook – opt for a menu which you will tackle with confidence.
- Ease of serving and eating the food: the only thing worse than a host or hostess who is overstretched by last-minute cooking between courses at a formal dinner party is the poor guest who is struggling with a knife and fork while standing and balancing a plate, glass and napkin, at the same time chatting politely to other guests.

COOKING IN QUANTITY

It is vital to select a menu which is manageable kitchen-wise and to batch cook ahead, if possible, to avoid running out of oven space, cooking utensils or equipment for one massive cooking session.

The following are all practical choices for buffets for large numbers up to fifty (or more), for informal parties or occasions such as weddings. The dishes selected may either be cooked ahead and frozen or they are a sensible choice for same-day cooking. Remember that you can hire large cooking pans for potatoes or rice that require last minute cooking. When batch baking these recipes, double the quantities; this is practical and speedy. The recipes suggested all feature in this book or a guide to proportions is included here. Consult the Index for page numbers.

Smoked Mackerel Pâté One quantity will serve 12 as part of a buffet. Freeze ahead.

Chicken Mayonnaise Allow 1 small boneless chicken breast per person, skinned. Roast, covered, cool and chill the day before. The chicken may be diced before chilling. Coat with mayonnaise thinned with a little cream or yogurt and dress with chopped parsley, chives and tarragon. For a well-dressed dish, allow 600 ml/1 pint mayonnaise and 300 ml/½ pint plain yogurt or cream for 25 chicken breasts. Browned flaked almonds or grated lemon rind may be sprinkled over instead of the herbs.

Baked Ham Order a whole cooked ham, preferably on the bone, from a good butcher, delicatessen or large supermarket. The rind may be removed and the fat coated with brown sugar, then browned in a hot oven before serving the ham.

Carbonnade of Beef Cook in double-quantity batches, with slightly less liquid; each batch to serve 12. Cool and freeze well ahead, packing in small quantities that thaw quickly. Thoroughly reheat in the oven just before serving the carbonnade.

New Potatoes Scrub and boil small new potatoes, then drain and toss in butter with chives or mint. They should be scrubbed the day before, boiled early on the day of the party until only just cooked, then drained and tossed in butter. Cool quickly and reheat well in their butter before serving. Allow 1.8–2.25 kg/4–5 lb for 16–20 portions; 5.5–6.75 kg/12–15 lb for 50 portions.

For a delicious salad, cook the potatoes completely, drain them thoroughly, then toss them in an oil and vinegar dressing, adding lots of snipped chives and chopped parsley. Cover and cool.

Cooked Rice Allow 50 g/2 oz per person as a side dish, 75 g/3 oz per person as part of a main dish (for example, risotto) on a buffet. Cook with twice the volume of water. If serving hot, cook ahead, cool and

chill promptly. Reheat thoroughly to a high temperature in covered serving dishes and serve promptly: do not reheat more than once and do not allow to stand, lukewarm, on the buffet for long periods. Rice salads should be kept chilled until served.

Quiche Make, chill and freeze quiches in advance, allowing 10–12 portions from a 20–23 cm/8–9 inch round quiche, depending on other food. Thaw and reheat just before serving.

Salad Green salad is practical and a refreshing accompaniment to most buffet food; however, it is seldom eaten in any quantity. Select a crisp lettuce and shred or cut all ingredients finely. A salad of 1 large lettuce, with cucumber, spring onions and green pepper will yield up to 30 portions as part of a buffet. Serve dressing separately.

Meringues Make ahead – when thoroughly dried, meringues keep well in airtight containers in a cool place for at least a couple of weeks. Pile them high in a dish and serve with a bowl each of whipped cream and strawberries for a 'do-it-yourself' dessert. Allow 600 ml/1 pint cream, whipped, to serve 15–20 and offer 75 g/3 oz strawberries per portion.

ADAPTING RECIPES

There are a number of important factors to bear in mind when catering in quantity. If you are planning to scale up a favourite recipe, you must first look at it carefully to see if it contains any strong flavourings. These do not need to be scaled up in the same proportions as the meat or vegetable content of the recipe, as a small amount of flavouring will penetrate quite large quantities of food. Spices, garlic, herbs, and strong seasonings all need to be handled with care.

The liquid content of the dish also needs to be looked at carefully. A fish dish with sauce, for example, will not need as much sauce when produced in quantity. Stews and casseroles, too, may not need the same proportion of liquid.

Apart from the logical reasons for these differences when increasing quantities, there is also a psychological factor. When dishes are prepared for four or six people, the cook wishes the food not only to be sufficient but to look sufficient, and very often enough food is made for five or seven. Unless this factor is taken into account when scaling up, the resultant recipe for fifty would actually feed sixty or more.

APPROXIMATE QUANTITIES OF BASIC FOODS PER PERSON

Bread	*French bread* 2 slices (with dinner; maybe more with salad); 3–4 slices (with just wine and cheese) *Rolls* 2
Cheese	100 g/4 oz (served at wine and cheese party); 50 g/2 oz (served as last course of dinner)
Meat	*On the bone* 150–225 g/5–8 oz (main course: depending on whether casseroled with vegetables or on its own) *Off the bone* 100–150 g/4–5 oz (main course: depending on whether casseroled with vegetables or on its own)
Chicken	*On the bone* 150–225 g/5–8 oz (main course: depending on whether casseroled with vegetables or on its own) *Off the bone* 100–150 g/4–5 oz (main course: depending on whether casseroled with vegetables or on its own)
Fish	*Fillet or steak* 100–150 g/4–5 oz (depending on whether main or subsidiary course)
Vegetables	100 g/4 oz (served with one other vegetable and potatoes as accompaniment to main course)
Rice	25–50 g/1–2 oz (uncooked)
Pasta	50–100 g/2–4 oz (depending on whether main course or subsidiary)
Gravy/sauces	75–100 ml/3–3½ fl oz (served with main dish)
Desserts	*Ice cream* 50–75 ml/2–3 fl oz (depending on richness, whether an accompaniment, etc) *Fruit* 150 g/5 oz (for fruit salad); *Pouring cream* 75 ml/3 fl oz
Tea	5 ml/1 tsp tea leaves per person; 125 ml/4 fl oz milk for 4 people
Coffee	125 ml/4 fl oz per person; 125 ml/4 fl oz cream for 4 people

Table Laying –
Dining in Style

*F*ollowing dining trends and fashions, there are many ways of laying the table, from formal settings to casual, yet attractive presentations, and the choice depends on the occasion.

PLACE SETTINGS

If soup is to be served, round soup spoons or dessertspoons should be provided. Special fish knives and forks can be laid for the fish course; the knives are blunt with a slightly pointed end which enables the bones to be eased out of the fish without cutting the flesh. Large knives and forks are laid for the main meat course, with a small knife for bread and butter and cheese. Steak knives with a serrated cutting edge are often used for grilled steak or chops. A dessertspoon and fork are provided for the sweet course, or a teaspoon if the dessert is to be served in small dishes. If fruit is served, knives and forks should be provided.

TABLE DECORATIONS

Flower arrangements should be low and the scent must not be overpowering. Candles should match table linen and/or room decor. Red wine should be placed ready on the sideboard or side table; white wine should be chilled. Remember to include a jug of iced water and soft drinks. Sauceboats should have a stand or saucer to avoid drips on the tablecloth.

THE BUFFET TABLE

The art of laying a buffet table is to show off the food to its best advantage while making serving easy.

For buffets to serve 50 people or more, place plates and cutlery at either end of the buffet table so that there are at least two serving points. This means that there must be two platters (at least) of each dish so that guests can help themselves from either end of the table. Drinks, and later coffee, should be served from a side table. Depending on the space available, the dessert can be displayed ready on a side table, or served from the main table when the main course is finished. Use cake stands for gâteau-type desserts to vary the height of the display. The most convenient way to lay cutlery is to wrap a set for each person in a table napkin. Distribute cruets along the table, and accompaniments (salad dressing or sauce) near the appropriate dishes. Place bread or rolls with butter at both ends of the table. Cheeseboards should be brought in with the dessert and placed at either end of the buffet with celery, biscuits and butter, and, of course, small plates and knives. For small buffets, it is usually possible to lay everything on one table with cutlery and plates at one end only.

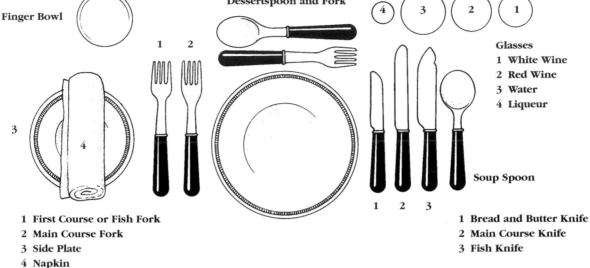

Finger Bowl

Dessertspoon and Fork

Glasses
1 White Wine
2 Red Wine
3 Water
4 Liqueur

Soup Spoon

1 First Course or Fish Fork
2 Main Course Fork
3 Side Plate
4 Napkin

1 Bread and Butter Knife
2 Main Course Knife
3 Fish Knife

TRADITIONAL FORMAL SETTINGS

Lay the knives, blades pointing inwards, on the right of the dinner plate and the forks on the left in the order in which they will be used (first to be used on the extreme right or left and the last next to the plate). The dessertspoon and fork can either be laid in neat alignment across the top of the setting, with the spoon handle to the right and the fork handle to the left, or at the sides of the plate, spoon on the right, fork on the left; either arrangement is correct. Fruit knives and forks can be laid across the top of the setting with the dessertspoon and fork, or at the side. Alternatively, they can be handed round with the dessert plates. The small knife for bread may go next to the dinner plate, on the right-hand side or vertically across the side plate, which should be on the left of the place setting. The soup spoon is placed on the extreme right-hand side as this is the first implement to be used. Line up the cutlery neatly and as close together as is practical, with the handles about 1 cm/½ inch from the edge of the table.

Glasses should be arranged in a straight line across the top of the right-hand cutlery, in the order of use; for example, a glass for white wine on the right, then one for red, and a port or liqueur glass on the left of the row. If you include a tumbler or stemmed glass for

water, place this before the liqueur glass. The last glass should be placed just above the meat knife. If only a single wine glass is to be used, put it anywhere above the right-hand cutlery.

If finger-bowls are provided, place these to the left just above the line of forks. Table napkins can be put in the centre of the place setting, on the side plate or in one of the glasses.

ALTERNATIVE SETTINGS

A completely different approach to table laying is sometimes suitable for casual or everyday entertaining. Place mats are widely used instead of tablecloths, on both formal and more relaxed occasions. The table setting may be changed completely to reflect the food, as when Chinese bowls, chopsticks, spoons and forks replace the traditional cutlery. For an informal, one-course meal, the cutlery (usually a knife and fork) may be placed neatly together on a napkin on the side plate in the centre of the setting. Match bright china with colourful napkins, flowers or ribbons to emphasize the light-hearted approach.

CUTLERY AND CONDIMENTS

Whatever the type of meal, always have the necessary serving utensils on the table.

Traditionally, serving spoons and forks are paired at both ends of the table, according to the number of dishes, arranged as for the dessert cutlery. Have all the implements for serving the main course on the table; those for the dessert may be brought in later.

Salt and pepper, or just a pepper mill, and any other condiments or accompaniments, should be positioned centrally but to one side of the table. For a large dinner party, it is customary to have more than one set of condiments and two plates of butter, each with its own butter knife.

NAPKIN FOLDING

Crisply starched and folded napkins may be left very plain, in large squares on the centre of each setting or folded on a side plate. Here are a couple of alternative ideas:

The Fan

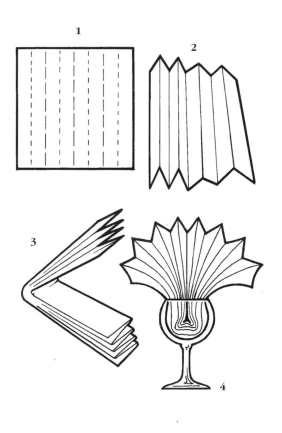

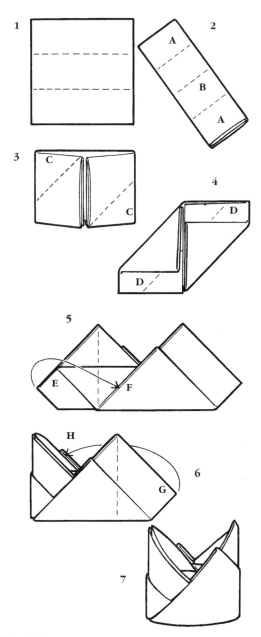

The Mitre

1 Fold the napkin into three
2 Fold ends (AA) over to centre line (B)
3 Fold corners (CC) to the centre
4 Fold the back across at dotted line (D)
5 Tuck point (E) into pleat (F)
6 Tuck point (G) into pleat (H) on the reverse side
7 Complete

Food Presentation – A Visual Feast

*G*ood food deserves pleasing presentation as well as careful cooking. The level of attention to presentation depends on the occasion; however, all food should look appetizing, from the simplest snack of cheese on toast to the most elaborate dinner party dish.

The food should be freshly prepared and neatly arranged, either on an individual plate or dish, or in a serving vessel. Avoid spilling food or sauces over the edge of a dish and do not pile food unattractively or mix separate items which are served together. Always adopt a neat approach to food, even when doing something simple like slicing or buttering bread, laying bacon rashers on a plate or cutting a wedge of cake, and the majority of your meals will automatically look good. A sloppy approach to basic techniques will give sloppy results and inferior appearance or, worse, a dish whose only decorative element is the garnish or decoration.

Garnishes and decorations are added to improve the overall appearance of the food; to add colour, a

contrasting texture and interest. Plain food will usually require a simple garnish, whereas a complicated dish can carry off a more elaborate arrangement. To a certain extent these touches are subject to fashion but there are a few useful rules to remember regardless of the current trend.

• The garnish or decoration must complement the food in terms of texture and flavour, as well as appearance.

• The finishing touches should be edible. In many instances garnishes may be herbs which are not necessarily eaten, but they should reflect the ingredients used in the dish. The best garnishes taste good with the food, the worst are a redundant nuisance on the plate.

• Sweet decorations should taste good as well as improve the appearance of the food.

• Garnishes and decorations should be prepared in advance as far as possible to avoid keeping hot food waiting before serving. They should be covered and kept cool or chilled.

• Except for decorative finishes that form an integral part of a dish, for example the coating or piping on a gâteau, the garnish or decoration should be added to the food just before serving, so that it looks its best.

CUTTING TECHNIQUES

Almost invariably, a small, fine-bladed, very sharp knife is all you need to cut garnishes successfully. This gives good results with even the most fiddly cuts. The following techniques are used for both savoury and sweet dishes. Remember to wash (and dry) garnishing ingredients, where appropriate, before use.

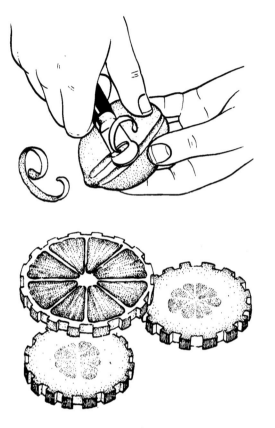

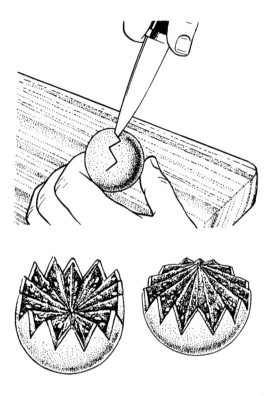

Using a Canelle Knife This is appropriate on citrus fruit, cucumber, courgettes or other ingredients with peel. Pare strips in a lengthways direction so that a fine, cog-wheel effect is achieved when the food is sliced.

Although a canelle knife simplifies this technique, a fine-bladed knife may be used with a slow, steady and even cutting motion. To remove narrow channels using a knife, cut 'V' shapes down the length of the fruit or vegetable.

Long fine strips of citrus rind may be cooked in simmering water until tender, then drained and used as a garnish or decoration.

Vandyke Technique For tomatoes, radishes, citrus fruit or any firm ingredient which is halved.

Use a fine-bladed knife. Holding food firmly by top and bottom, cut in towards the centre all around the middle, making 'V' shaped cuts, then gently ease the two halves apart.

Vandyke-cut fruit may be used as a base for serving sorbets or ice creams. The fruit may be scooped out of the peel and the shell used as a container. For example, lemon shells may be filled with fish pâtés or mousses, or with lemon sorbet.

A Vandyked watermelon, filled with a colourful fruit salad, including watermelon balls, makes a wonderful centrepiece for a buffet table.

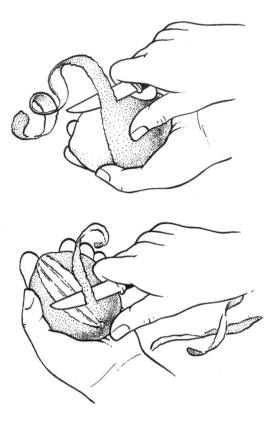

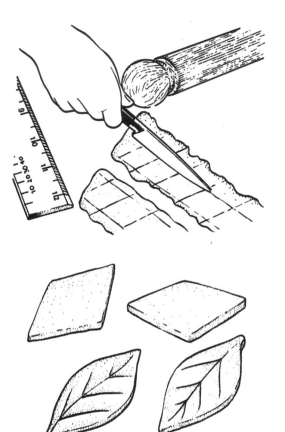

Paring Many garnishes involve thinly paring strips off food, or removing peel. Use a small sharp knife and cut slowly but evenly to ensure that the strip is very thin. Strips may be peeled in a straight direction, usually lengthways off fruit or vegetables, or they may be cut in a spiral, around the food. Spiral strips may be rolled to represent roses, or cut into fine, curled strips.

Pared citrus rind is often used to flavour and decorate drinks. Orange rind may be added to mulled wine; lemon and lime rind are excellent for fruit punches or cocktails.

Pared citrus rind can also be wound up tightly and inserted into a bottle of wine vinegar or into a container of salad dressing. If left for several days, the rind imparts its flavour to the vinegar or dressing.

Cutting Decorative Shapes Leaves, flowers or other shapes may be cut from sliced fruit and vegetables, fruit or vegetable peel, pastry and other ingredients, such as chocolate or aspic.

Freehand cutting produces pleasing original results, whereas the use of cutters gives uniform shapes. Use a clean ruler (kept for the purpose) to cut geometric shapes and strips. Leaves may be cut by marking veins on diamond shapes. As a compromise between freehand and cutters, prepare diamond shapes for leaves, then round off the shapes slightly using the point of a knife.

CLASSIC GARNISHES

Fresh Herbs These add colour and interest. They should also provide the diner with an indication of the flavour of the dish. Wash and dry sprigs well and use them in moderation, usually on serving dshes. Parsley is a popular garnish but it can be an irritating extra when it is totally superfluous and unrelated to the ingredients it supposedly enhances. Other herbs used for garnishing include coriander, dill, basil, chervil, fennel and borage.

Fried Parsley The classic garnish for fried fish. Thoroughly wash and dry neat, fresh parsley sprigs. Deep fry in hot oil for a few seconds until bright green and crisp. Drain on absorbent kitchen paper.

Salad Leaves Watercress or mustard and cress are typical garnishes. These must be perfectly fresh and crisp. Shredded lettuce, rocket, celery leaves and other salad leaves all make attractive garnishes with the right foods. They complement grilled and fried foods; also boiled hams, quiches and pies, but do not go well with sauced dishes.

If the salad garnish is intended to be eaten, spoon a little French-type dressing over it just before serving. If you do not want to add an oil and vinegar dressing, trickle a few drops of walnut or hazelnut oil and a little fresh lemon juice over.

Salad Vegetables Tomatoes, cucumber, radishes and other vegetables that are generally eaten raw in salad contribute colour and texture when used as a garnish for hot or cold dishes. Add them to cold sauced foods, such as chaudfroid dishes and mayonnaise-dressed foods, or use them with grills and fried foods.

Cooked Vegetables A mixture of blanched diced root vegetables, known as a *macedoine,* is a classic garnish for fish, poultry and meat dishes. Deep-fried, very thinly sliced potatoes (crisps or game chips) are a traditional accompaniment and garnish for game. Thin sticks – or julienne – of colourful vegetables, like carrots and leek, are blanched and arranged in neat piles as a garnish for fish, poultry or meat dishes, particularly those served coated with sauce (see also page 16). Grilled tomatoes are often served with grilled meat.

DECORATIVE TECHNIQUES WITH VEGETABLES

Tomato Roses Use a small, sharp pointed knife to thinly pare a strip of peel and flesh from the outside of a ripe tomato. Cut around the fruit in a spiral, then arrange the strip of peel in a neat rosette to represent a rose.

The peel from yellow tomatoes and persimmons (or Sharon fruit) can be removed using this technique and rolled to make yellow or orange-red roses.

Spring Onion Curls Trim a spring onion, then make slits down the green part to shred the onion, leaving the fine pieces attached at the white end. Place in a bowl of iced water for at least 30 minutes. The shreds will curl.

This curling technique may also be used for celery, by shredding a length of celery stick, leaving the pieces attached at the end of the stick.

Radish Roses Make small 'V' cuts all around the base of a radish, then carefully pare off the vegetable from the point of the 'V' downwards, leaving each piece attached at the base in the form of a petal. Work more rows of cuts around the radish, from the base up towards the top. Then place the radish in a bowl of iced water and leave to stand for at least 30 minutes, or longer. The roses will open.

The technique can be adapted to make curved petals by cutting semi-circles downwards into the radishes instead of cutting 'V' shapes.

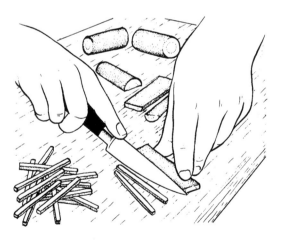

Julienne Cut thin slices of vegetable, then cut neat fine sticks, each about 2.5–5 cm/1–2 inches long. Depending on the vegetable, the julienne may be blanched before use. A combination of vegetables, such as carrot and leek, makes an attractive garnish.

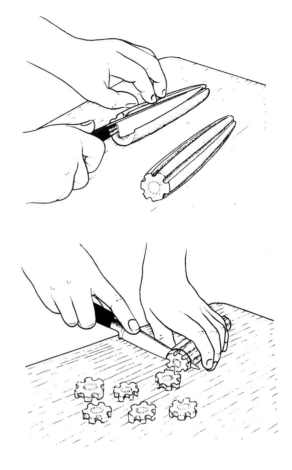

Vegetable Flowers or Shapes Prepared, sliced vegetables should be parboiled until tender before being cut in decorative shapes. Use aspic cutters to stamp flowers or shapes out of the vegetables. Carrots, turnips, potatoes and swedes are all suitable. Shapes can also be stamped from salad vegetables, such as cucumber or large white radishes, although these should not be cooked.

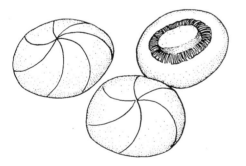

Turned Mushrooms Use small, perfect button mushrooms. Using a small pointed knife, cut off thin, narrow strips of peel from the centre of the mushroom outwards to the edge of the cap. Shape the cuts in spirals.

A canelle knife (page 13) can be used to cut the spiral shapes into slightly larger, closed cap mushrooms.

Carrot Flowers Use a small, pointed knife to carve the outside of a carrot into petals. Simple but highly effective flowers may be made by simply cutting fine 'V' strips lengthways out of the carrot, then slicing the carrot thinly and blanching the slices in boiling water. This technique can be used when preparing vegetables for a dinner party. The carrot trimmings can be used to flavour stock or soup.

DECORATIVE TECHNIQUES WITH FRUIT

Lemon Twists Use this technique for lemon, lime or small orange slices. Cut thin slices of fruit (not so thin that they flop). Make a cut from the centre of the slice outwards, then twist the fruit.

Pared Citrus Rind Pare the rind thinly from the fruit, then cut it into fine strips. Simmer the strips in water until tender, then drain well. Use with fish, meat or vegetables as well as with sweet dishes.

DAIRY GARNISHES

Eggs and cream are classic garnishing ingredients. Slices or wedges of hard-boiled egg are simple options; alternatively, separate the yolk and white, then chop both. This is a classic garnish.

Quails' eggs are excellent for garnishing canapés and first courses: fresh eggs should be boiled for about 4 minutes, then drained and shelled. Pickled quails' eggs are a good storecupboard standby for adding an impromptu garnish to salads and savoury mousses or cold savoury soufflés which can look disappointingly bland. The eggs may be used whole, halved or sliced.

Swirling Cream Swirl single or whipping cream into sauces or soup just before serving. Use a small jug with a good pouring spout or a spoon to pour the cream into soup. Pour the cream in a 'C' shape, then drag it around into a swirl using a cocktail stick, skewer or fine pointed knife.

To swirl cream through a sauce on a plate, drop teaspoonfuls of cream in streaks into the sauce, then drag them, using a cocktail stick.

For a feathered effect, drop small dots of cream from the tip of a teaspoon, then drag a cocktail stick just once through the middle of each dot.

These techniques also work with yogurt and fromage frais.

Swirling Cream

Feathering Cream

BREAD AND PASTRY GARNISHES

Apart from adding the finishing touches to pastry dishes, pastry garnishes may be added to a variety of dishes, including soups and stews.

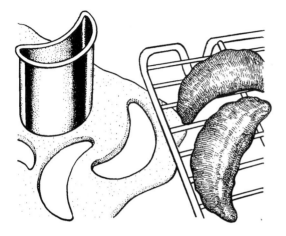

Fleurons These small crescents of puff pastry, glazed with egg and baked until puffed and golden, are usually served with soup, stews or sauced dishes. They may also add a pleasing contrast in texture to some salads and first courses.

Buttered Crumbs Fresh breadcrumbs, fried in butter or a mixture of oil and butter until crisp and golden, may be sprinkled over sauced, poached or steamed food. A little chopped parsley or lemon rind may be added.

Croûtons Small bread cubes, traditionally no more than 1 cm/½ inch in size, fried in a mixture of butter and oil until crisp and golden, make a classic soup garnish. Turn the cubes often during cooking for even browning. Drain on absorbent kitchen paper.

Croûtes These are pieces of fried bread, (usually slices cut in triangles or rounds) larger than croûtons. They may be arranged as a border for casseroles or stews, sauced dishes or gratins. They are also used as a base for serving foods such as roast game or fillet steaks, the object being to capture the juices in the bread. In modern cookery, croûtes are sometimes toasted rather than fried.

Pastry Shapes Use decorative cutters to stamp out shapes in puff or short crust pastry. Glaze with egg before baking.

DECORATIONS FOR DESSERTS

By their very nature, desserts demand attractive presentation, especially when served at parties or other festive occasions. From the elegance of an ice bowl to the sophistication of a black ribbon tied around the dish holding a coffee soufflé, sweet decorations provide the perfect opportunity for exercising artistic skills.

Making Ice Bowls Bowls of ice are the perfect vessels for serving ice creams or sorbets. They may also be used to hold fresh fruit such as strawberries, or fruit salads that are not heavily coated in syrup.

Ice bowls may be large or small, depending on the size of the bowls you use to set them. Make an ice bowl at least a day before you intend to use it. If used with care, the bowl may be replaced in the freezer and stored for use on another occasion. Individual ice bowls are particularly attractive and can be made using small freezer containers.

You will need two freezerproof bowls, one about 7.5 cm/3 inches larger in diameter than the other. Pour cold water into the larger bowl to two-thirds fill it. In the sink, put the smaller bowl into the larger one and weight it down so that its base is about 4 cm/1½ inches above the base of the outer bowl. Use masking tape, or heavy parcel tape, to keep the small bowl floating in the middle of the water in the outer bowl. Clear a suitable space in the freezer and freeze the bowls. Alternatively, some kitchenware suppliers sell 'double' bowls especially designed for making ice bowls.

As the water freezes, flower petals and leaves may be pushed down into it. Use a skewer to tease these into place. When the ice bowl has frozen solid, remove the weights and tape. Lift out the small bowl – if it is stuck, simply pour in a little hot water to loosen it.

Dip the outer bowl in hot water to loosen the ice bowl, then put it in the freezer until the dessert is to be served. Ice creams or other frozen desserts which are to be served in the ice bowl may be arranged in it in advance and kept in the freezer for a couple of hours.

Simple Decorative Touches If you do not have the perfect serving dish for a particular dessert, transform a plain dish by adding a bow of ribbon. Ovenproof glass dishes, plain white serving dishes or soufflé dishes, or even inexpensive glass dishes look far better with a piece of wide ribbon around the outside, tied in a

flamboyant bow. Set the dish on a large dinner plate lined with a doily.

Frosted Rims This decorative touch is more often used for cocktail glasses but looks good with ice creams or sorbets. Use fine glass dessert dishes, wine glasses or cocktail glasses. Have a saucer of water and a saucer of caster sugar at the ready. The water may be coloured with a few drops of food colouring if you like – for example pink to go with a pink-coloured dessert or green to complement a lime, grape or mint ice cream. Dip the rim of the glass in the saucer of water, then dip it into the sugar. Hold the glass upside down for a few seconds to allow any excess moisture or sugar to drop off. Fill the glass carefully.

Piping with Fresh Cream Swirls of cream make gâteaux, moulded desserts, trifles and sundaes look particularly luscious. Piping decorations with fresh cream is not difficult if you remember a few basic rules.

When whipping cream, a balloon whisk gives the most volume but using it can be hard work. A rotary or electric whisk is quicker. When using an electric mixer it is important not to overwhip the cream. The cream is ready when it stands in soft, smooth peaks and just holds its shape. As you pipe the cream it tends to thicken very slightly. Cream that is overwhipped has a grainy, slightly curdled appearance.

Use a large nozzle for piping fresh cream. Large star nozzles, or Savoy nozzles, are suitable. Large nozzles with lots of small serrations around the edge are also available. Fit the nozzle into a clean plastic or fabric piping bag. Keep all the utensils and your hands as cool as possible. If your hands are very warm, the cream will thicken and become slightly buttery as you pipe it.

To pipe swirls, hold the bag vertically above the position on the dessert and squeeze gently, turning the bag around to create a large or small swirl. Lift the nozzle away sharply to give a point. When piping large swirls on a round dessert, start by piping four on opposite sides, then fill in the spaces between.

To pipe shells or scrolls, hold the nozzle at an angle of about 60° to the top of the dessert. For a clean, flat edge at the end of a line of shells, cut the cream away from the nozzle with the blade of a knife after piping. Pipe a small star to neaten a join in a border of shells or scrolls.

FINISHING TOUCHES WITH FRUIT

• Fresh fruit makes an excellent decoration for a wide variety of desserts. Slices, segments or small whole fruit may be added to the top of a dessert. Alternatively, add fruit to the rim of a serving dish or stand a bowl on a large plate and decorate the plate with fruit.

• Thin slices of orange or lemon may be used either whole, halved or cut into quarters. Cut into the centre of a slice, then twist the cut edges outwards to make a twist.

• Slices of exotic fruit, such as star fruit or kiwi fruit, are particularly attractive. Overlap them around the edge of a trifle or on the top of a cheesecake.

• Pare off long, fine strips of rind from an orange or lemon. Cut these into shreds and cook them in a little simmering water for about 5 minutes, or until tender. Drain and dry the shreds on absorbent kitchen paper before sprinkling or mounding them on a dessert.

• Grapes, cherries, strawberries, Cape gooseberries, raspberries or mandarin segments may all be frosted. Brush the fruit with a little water, then roll it in caster sugar. Dry on a wire rack.

CHOCOLATE DECORATIONS

Dark and bitter, smooth and milky or pale and creamy: there are many types of chocolate available now and they can be put to a wide variety of decorative uses. Use a hard, plain dessert chocolate for the best flavour and texture. Do not be disappointed by the appearance of chocolate decorations: they will not have the same high gloss as commercial chocolates. Avoid handling the chocolate decorations once set as fingermarks will readily show and the surface will become dull.

A block of chocolate can be finely or coarsely grated, chopped, slivered and curled for decorating or coating the sides and tops of cakes. Melted chocolate has many uses: it can be poured over cakes, or fruits, marzipan and nuts can be dipped in it. Chocolate leaves are made by coating real leaves. Chocolate curls, known as caraque, are a widely used decoration. Melted chocolate can also be set in a thin sheet, then cut into shapes, for example squares, triangles or shapes using cutters. The melted chocolate can also be piped through a small greaseproof paper (or parchment) piping bag which has just its point snipped off.

Store chocolate decorations in a cool, dry atmosphere for the shortest possible time, and no longer than seven to ten days. Chocolate will sweat if it is kept in a warm room. On very hot days keep the chocolate in the refrigerator but bring it to room temperature before melting it.

Chocolate Shapes Spread melted chocolate in a thin even layer over a marble slab. When set, use cocktail cutters to stamp out shapes. Alternatively, cut out squares or triangles.

Chocolate Leaves Paint melted chocolate over clean, dry rose leaves. Leave until set, then peel away the leaves from the chocolate.

Chocolate Caraque Pour melted chocolate on to a marble slab and leave to set. Use a large kitchen knife to scrape long curls off the chocolate. To do this, hold both ends of the knife's blade and slide it across the chocolate at an acute angle.

Chocolate Cups Make small chocolate cups in which to serve ices or individual fruit salads. Alternatively, the chocolate cups may be filled with mousse or trifle mixture: brush the inside of double-thick paper cake cases thinly with melted chocolate, allowing each successive layer to dry before adding the next, until a thick even case is created. Keep cool. Remove the paper cases just before serving the chocolate cups.

Chocolate Shapes

Chocolate Leaves

Chocolate Caraque

Chocolate Cups

Chopping Chocolate Break the chocolate into pieces and place it on a chopping board. Use a sharp knife with a long blade and hold the tip of the knife on to the board with one hand. Pivot the blade, bringing it up and down with the other hand. Scrape the chocolate back to the centre of the board and continue until the pieces are even and quite small.

Grating Chocolate Place the grater on a piece of greaseproof paper on a large plate or chopping board. Rub the block of chocolate on the coarse side of the grater. Use long, even strokes and keep your hands as cool as possible.

Chocolate Slivers Hold your hands under cold running water, then dry them. Hold the chocolate in the palm of the hand and shave off thin pieces of chocolate with a potato peeler, letting them fall on to a chilled plate or a sheet of greaseproof paper or parchment.

Melted Chocolate Break up or roughly chop the chocolate and place it in a bowl that fits over a saucepan. Place about 5 cm/2 inches of water in the pan and bring it to the boil, then remove the pan from the heat and stand the bowl over it. Leave for a few minutes, then stir the chocolate until it has melted and is smooth and glossy. If you leave the pan on the heat, the chocolate will overheat and white streaks may appear in it when it sets again.

DIPPING FOOD IN CHOCOLATE

Biscuits, choux buns, nuts, marzipan shapes, real leaves and fruits such as maraschino cherries, grapes, raisins, dates and slices of banana can all be dipped in melted chocolate. They can be part-dipped or fully dipped according to the effect required. Special dipping forks have two long prongs that are bent at the ends to stop the food falling off when dipped. Alternatively, use a corn-on-the-cob fork, cocktail stick or two fine skewers, one on either side of the food. For larger pieces of food such as choux buns, or hard foods such as almonds, it is best to use your fingers for dipping.

Melt the chocolate following the instructions left. For dipping food the consistency should be thick enough to coat the back of a spoon. If the chocolate is too thin, remove the bowl from the pan and leave it to cool slightly, until the chocolate thickens. Keep the chocolate warm (over the saucepan of water), while you are working. If the chocolate becomes too thick, remove the bowl, reheat the water, then replace the bowl. Stir the chocolate occasionally as you are dipping the food; this gives a glossy finish.

You will need a good depth of melted chocolate to dip food successfully; it should be at least 5 cm/ 2 inches deep. (When the chocolate becomes too shallow for successful dipping, do not discard it; stir the excess into buttercreams or similar icings to avoid wastage.)

Line a baking sheet or wire rack with a sheet of waxed paper or non-stick baking parchment. Have ready all the food to be dipped and start with firm items, such as nuts and marzipan. Finish with soft foods, such as fruits. Plunge the food into the chocolate to the depth required, then quickly withdraw it at the same angle at which it was plunged. Do not rotate part-dipped food in the chocolate or the top line of chocolate will be uneven. Gently shake the food to allow the excess chocolate to fall back into the bowl, then place it on the prepared sheet or rack to dry.

PIPING CHOCOLATE

When adding chocolate decoration to the top of a cake, melted chocolate is difficult to pipe because it begins to set in the nozzle. Mixing a little icing sugar with it will make it more malleable; however this is not suitable for piping shapes that have to set hard. Stir 25 g/1 oz sifted icing sugar into 100 g/4 oz melted chocolate with a few drops of water to make a mixture of a thick piping consistency that drops from the spoon.

Menus for Sharing and Celebrating

*M*rs Beeton wrote extensively on dinners and dining and provided her readers
with seasonal menus for all occasions. Her advice to readers
includes the observation:

'Dinner, being the grand solid meal of the day, is a matter of considerable importance;
and a well-served table is a striking index of human ingenuity and resource.'

*Her menus were invaluable to young ladies who had never cooked a morsel, yet,
once married and running their own households, were faced with the prospect of
intelligently discussing celebration meals with their cooks. Having quoted from
great diners, Isabella Beeton was, as ever, entirely practical:*

'Leaving great men of all kinds, however, to get their own dinners, let us, who are
not great, look after ours. Dine we must, and we may as well dine elegantly as well
as wholesomely.'

A meal that combines a late breakfast with an early lunch is the perfect way to begin the day with house guests.

Menu for Eight

PORRIDGE WITH HONEY AND
CLOTTED CREAM
.....
ORANGE AND GRAPEFRUIT
SALAD
GREEN FRUIT SALAD
TROPICAL FRUIT SALAD
.....
KEDGEREE
BACON ROLLS
.....
BREADS
PRESERVES

The dishes on this menu complement each other to make a hearty meal or may be eaten individually as a lighter snack. Offering a choice of fruit salads is a good idea when serving a special-occasion brunch, or you may prefer to make a large quantity of a single salad. Offer a large bowl of Greek yogurt or crème fraîche with the fruit salads.

Serve jugs of orange juice, keep the kettle boiling to brew tea as needed and ensure that there is a constant supply of aromatic coffee. Bucks fizz – a mixture of Champagne or dry sparkling white wine and orange juice – brings a sparkle to a special occasion.

Arrange a selection of sweet preserves on the table, such as marmalade, apricot jam and cherry preserve, and offer dishes of butter and/or a substitute spread.

PERFECT PORRIDGE

A steaming pan of creamy porridge will stay at just the right temperature when placed on a candle warmer. To make traditional porridge for eight, you will need 1.75 litres/3 pints water and 350 g/12 oz rolled oats. Stir the oats into the water in a large heavy-bottomed saucepan and add 2.5–5 ml/½–1 tsp salt. Stir over moderate heat until the porridge boils, then reduce the heat and cook the mixture very gently, stirring occasionally, for 10 minutes. Serve with honey and clotted cream. Single cream and brown sugar may be offered if preferred.

BACON ROLLS

Crisp bacon rolls are easy to prepare, smell wonderful as they cook and are delicious with kedgeree or simply as a savoury snack with fresh bread. Streaky bacon is ideal for crisp rolls; back bacon is the leaner choice. Remove the rind and any small pieces of bone, if necessary, roll up each rasher neatly, then thread it on to a metal skewer. Arrange the skewers in in the grill pan, or place them in a roasting tin to go in the oven.

Grill the bacon rolls, turning the skewers once or twice, until they are crisp and brown all over. If you prefer to bake the rolls, cook them in a preheated oven at 220°C/425°F/gas 7 for about 20 minutes. Use a fork to slide the bacon rolls off the skewers and serve them on a clean napkin or folded absorbent kitchen paper in a warmed dish.

MORNING BREAD BASKET

Bake or buy a selection of breads, including some unusual varieties and a range of shapes. To provide plenty of choice, buy more breads than you strictly need; leftovers will freeze well.

Crisp breakfast rolls, muffins (ready for splitting and toasting) and soda bread are all ideal for serving with savoury dishes as well as sweet preserves. Croissants, brioches and currant buns add a suggestion of sweetness, and, for guests who enjoy toothsome treats, fresh Danish pastries or doughnuts may be offered.

Orange and Grapefruit Salad

Ortaniques would make a delicious addition to this salad. These juicy citrus fruits are a cross between a tangerine and an orange. Their thin skins make them very easy to peel and segment.

SERVES 6

4 oranges
2 pink grapefruit
SYRUP
225 g/8 oz sugar
30 ml/2 tbsp orange liqueur

Using a vegetable peeler, remove all the rind from 1 orange, taking care not to include any of the bitter pith. Cut the rind into strips with a sharp knife. Bring a small saucepan of water to the boil, add the orange strips and cook for 1 minute, then drain and set aside on absorbent kitchen paper.

Peel the remaining oranges and remove all the pith. Using a sharp knife, carefully cut between the segment membranes to remove the flesh. Work over a bowl to catch any juice, and squeeze out all the juice from the remaining pulp. Segment both the grapefruit in the same way.

Make the syrup. Put the sugar in a pan with 200 ml/ 7 fl oz water. Heat gently, stirring until the sugar has dissolved, then bring to the boil and boil rapidly, without stirring, until the syrup turns golden. Remove from the heat and carefully add the fruit juice and liqueur. Set aside to cool.

Arrange the citrus segments in concentric circles in a shallow serving dish or large quiche dish. Pour the caramel syrup over the top and chill thoroughly.

Green Fruit Salad

There is no need to stick precisely to the selection or the proportions of fruit in the recipe; simply remember that you will need a total of about 1 kg/2¼ lb. The fruit is traditionally served in syrup, as here, but fresh fruit juices, perhaps sparked with alcohol for an extra-special occasion, are equally popular today.

SERVES 4–6

175 g/6 oz green-fleshed melon, scooped into balls
175 g/6 oz seedless green grapes
2 Granny Smith apples
2 kiwi fruit, peeled and sliced
2 greengages, halved and stoned
2 passion fruit
mint sprigs to decorate
SYRUP
175 g/6 oz sugar
30 ml/2 tbsp lemon juice

Make the syrup. Put the sugar in a saucepan with 450 ml/¾ pint water. Heat gently, stirring until the sugar has dissolved, then bring to the boil and boil rapidly until the syrup has been reduced by about half. Add the lemon juice, allow to cool, then pour the syrup into a glass serving bowl.

When the syrup is quite cold, add the fruit. Leave the skin on the apples and either slice them or cut them into chunks. Cut the passion fruit in half and scoop out the pulp, straining it to remove the seeds, if preferred. Serve well chilled, decorated with mint.

Tropical Fruit Salad

SERVES 8

1 small pineapple
1 mango
1 (312 g/11 oz) can lychees, drained
1 (425 g/15 oz) can guava halves, drained
3 bananas
250 ml/8 fl oz tropical fruit juice

Peel the pineapple, removing the eyes. Cut in half or quarters lengthways and cut out the hard core. Cut the fruit into neat chunks and place in a serving dish.

Peel and slice the mango, discarding the stone. Add the mango flesh to the bowl with the lychees and guavas. Peel the bananas and slice them into the fruit salad. Pour over the tropical fruit juice and chill.

FRESH LYCHEES AND GUAVAS

Fresh lychees have a red, crisp coating and a large central stone and their white flesh is aromatic, juicy and bursting with flavour. To peel and stone lychees, slit the peel lengthways with a small sharp knife and it will easily slide off the fruit. Then slit the fruit lengthways and the stone can be slipped out without difficulty. Sometimes the flesh tends to cling to the stalk end of the stone, but it can be loosened with the point of a sharp knife.

Fresh, pear-shaped guavas are green or green-yellow in colour. They vary in size and their flavour can be disappointing when under-ripe. Treat these fruit like a pear: peel and quarter them lengthways, then cut out the core of seeds. Brush cut fresh guavas with a little lemon juice, or place them straight into the tropical fruit juice, as they discolour when exposed to air for long periods.

Kedgeree

SERVES 8

salt and pepper
300 g/10 oz long-grain rice
250 ml/8 fl oz milk
900 g/2 lb smoked haddock
75 g/3 oz butter
15 ml/1 tbsp curry powder
4 hard-boiled eggs, roughly chopped
cayenne pepper
GARNISH
25 g/1 oz butter
2 hard-boiled eggs, whites and yolks sieved separately
45 ml/3 tbsp chopped parsley

Bring a saucepan of salted water to the boil. Add the rice and cook for 12 minutes. Drain thoroughly, rinse under cold water and drain again. Place the strainer over a saucepan of simmering water to keep the rice warm while you cook the fish.

Put the milk in a large shallow saucepan or frying pan with 250 ml/8 fl oz water. Bring to simmering point, add the fish and poach gently for 4 minutes. Using a slotted spoon and a fish slice, transfer the haddock to a wooden board. Discard the cooking liquid in the pan.

Remove the skin and any bones from the haddock and break up the flesh into fairly large flakes. Melt half the butter in a large saucepan. Stir in the curry powder and cook it gently for 2–3 minutes, then add the flaked fish. Warm the mixture through. Remove from the heat, lightly stir in the chopped eggs, then add salt, pepper and cayenne to taste.

Melt the remaining butter in a second pan, add the rice and toss until well coated. Season lightly with salt, pepper and cayenne. Add the rice to the haddock mixture and mix well. Pile the kedgeree on to a warmed dish.

Dot the kedgeree with the butter, garnish with sieved hard-boiled egg yolk, egg white and parsley and serve at once.

A TRIO OF FRUIT SALADS

Three refreshing fruit salads set the tone for this stylish brunch menu which combines the best of traditional morning fare with lighter alternatives to revive after-party spirits.

> *W*hen the country-side is crisp with frost and a morning walk brings a glow of colour to the cheeks, a bowl of steaming hot soup makes the perfect lunch.

Menu for Six

ANCHOVY TOAST FINGERS

·····

MINESTRONE
HOME-BAKED BREAD ROLLS

·····

CHEESEBOARD
PICKLED ONIONS

·····

FRUIT BASKET

A brisk morning walk, a hearty lunch and an afternoon spent decking the Christmas tree makes a truly festive Saturday in December. This no-fuss menu is equally suitable for any wintry weekend.

The soup can be prepared the day before – its flavour will only improve – but do not add the pasta until reheating as it will swell and soften if the soup is left to stand for several hours. Prepare the anchovy butter in advance, so that it can be spread on hot toast and served as an appetizer while the soup is heating.

It is a good idea to make a batch of pickled onions in the autumn, ready for adding a little relish to cold suppers and bread-and-cheese lunches. Other pickles and chutneys may be served if preferred, such as pickled beetroot or red cabbage.

LUNCHTIME CHEESEBOARD

Hard British cheeses are the best choice for a plough-man's lunch. Select a good mature Cheddar and a Stilton, and balance these with a mild cheese, such as Cheshire or a nutty Double Gloucester. Here are a few additional or alternative suggestions:

Wensleydale A white, crumbly, close-textured cheese which is softer than a Cheddar. Slightly salty when young, this cheese is always mild. Blue Wensleydale has a stronger flavour and is more moist but is not as full-flavoured and creamy as blue Cheshire or a mature Stilton.

Sage Derby This is a good choice for a ploughman's lunch as it derives lots of flavour from the streaks of green sage that run through the cheese.

Red Windsor Flavoured with wine, this moist, mild Cheddar-style cheese has a distinctive red colour. Its cheese-and-wine-flavour goes well with warmed fresh crusty bread.

Cornish Yarg This firm, white cheese has a mild, almost tangy flavour. The cheese is enclosed in a dark, nettle crust. It provides a contrasting flavour to the buttery Cheddars on a British cheeseboard.

FRUIT TO SERVE WITH HARD CHEESE

A bowl of highly polished apples and pears looks good and both fruits will complement the hard cheeses perfectly.

Juicy seedless oranges, mandarins or clementines are in their prime during the winter months and are excellent in place of dessert.

DRINKS

Mulled cider or wine may be served with the anchovy toasts. Red wine is an obvious choice with the meal, but full-flavoured old ale is a good alternative. As well as regional ciders, a light, low-alcohol cider makes a refreshing change. Cider spritzers – cider topped up with sparkling mineral water – are also very thirst quenching.

FREEZING BREAD ROLLS

Make a batch of bread rolls well in advance, then freeze them in tightly sealed polythene bags. Take the rolls out of the freezer early in the morning and crisp them in a hot oven for 3–4 minutes before serving.

Anchovy Toast Fingers

SERVES 4–6

1 (50 g/2 oz) can anchovy fillets
100 g/4 oz butter, softened
cayenne pepper
prepared mustard
6–8 slices of toast

Pound the anchovies and their oil to a paste, then mix with the butter, adding a little cayenne and mustard to taste. Spread on hot toast, cut into neat fingers and serve at once.

Home-baked Bread Rolls

MAKES 24

fat for greasing
800 g/1¾ lb strong white flour
10 ml/2 tsp salt
25 g/1 oz lard
1 sachet fast-action easy-blend dried yeast
2.5 ml/½ tsp sugar
flour for kneading
beaten egg or milk for glazing
poppy seeds or sesame seeds for topping (optional)

Grease two baking trays. Sift the flour and salt into a large bowl. Rub in the lard. Stir in the yeast and sugar, then make a well in the middle of the dry ingredients. Add 500 ml/17 fl oz hand-hot water and gradually stir in the dry ingredients to make a soft dough. Turn on to a lightly floured surface and knead for about 8 minutes or until the dough is smooth, elastic and no longer sticky.

Divide the dough into 24 x 50 g/2 oz pieces and shape as shown on the right. Place the rolls on the greased baking sheets and cover them loosely with oiled polythene. Leave the rolls in a warm place until they have doubled in size.

Set the oven at 220°C/425°F/gas 7. Brush the risen rolls with beaten egg or milk. Leave the rolls plain or sprinkle them with poppy seeds or sesame seeds. Bake for 12–15 minutes, until well browned. Tap the bottom of one roll to check if the batch is cooked: it should sound hollow; if not cook the rolls for a further 3–5 minutes and check again.

FANCY ROLL SHAPES

Small Plaits Divide each piece of dough into three equal portions; then shape each of these into a long strand. Plait the strands together, pinching the ends securely.

Small Twists Divide each piece of dough into two equal portions, and shape into strands about 12 cm/4½ inches in length. Twist the strands together, pinching the ends securely.

'S' Rolls Shape each piece of dough into a roll about 15 cm/6 inches in length, and form it into an 'S' shape.

Cottage Rolls Cut two-thirds off each piece of dough and shape into a ball. Shape the remaining third in the same way. Place the small ball on top of the larger one and push a hole through the centre of both with one finger, dusted with flour, to join the two pieces firmly together.

Minestrone

SERVES 6

75 g/3 oz small haricot beans
15 ml/1 tbsp oil
2 rindless streaky bacon rashers, chopped
1 leek, trimmed, thinly sliced and washed
1 onion, chopped
1 garlic clove, crushed
2 carrots, thinly sliced
50 g/2 oz French beans, sliced
3 celery sticks, sliced
2 potatoes, diced
150 g/5 oz white cabbage, shredded
1 bay leaf
30 ml/2 tbsp tomato purée
1.25 litres/2¼ pints white stock
salt and pepper
50 g/2 oz small pasta shells or rings
grated Parmesan cheese to serve

Soak the beans overnight in water to cover. Next day, drain the beans and put them in a large saucepan with fresh water to cover. Bring to the boil, boil vigorously for 10 minutes, then drain thoroughly.

Heat the oil in a large saucepan, add the bacon, leek, onion and garlic and fry gently for about 10 minutes.

Add the remaining vegetables and cook, stirring frequently, for 2–3 minutes. Stir in the drained beans, with the bay leaf, tomato purée, stock and pepper. Do not add salt at this stage. Bring the soup to the boil, lower the heat, cover the pan and simmer for 45–60 minutes or until the haricot beans are tender. Add salt to taste.

Stir in the pasta and cook for 8–12 minutes or until tender but still firm to the bite. Remove the bay leaf. Serve the soup at once, sprinkled with Parmesan cheese.

PRESSURE COOKING SOUP

Minestrone can be made very successfully in the pressure cooker. Make the soup as suggested above, but do not add the cabbage with the other vegetables. Reduce the quantity of stock to 900 ml/1½ pints. Put the lid on and bring to 15 lb pressure. Cook for 10 minutes; reduce the pressure slowly. Add the cabbage and pasta, stirring well. Close the lid again, bring the soup back to 15 lb pressure and cook for 5 minutes more. Reduce the pressure slowly, remove the bay leaf and add salt to taste. Serve as suggested left.

Pickled Onions

MAKES ABOUT 1.4 KG/3 LB

450 g/1 lb salt
1.4 kg/3 lb pickling onions
2.25 litres/4 pints cold Spiced Vinegar (below)
5 ml/1 tsp mustard seeds (optional)

Dissolve half the salt in 2 litres/3½ pints of water in a large bowl. Add the onions. Set a plate inside the bowl to keep the onions submerged, weighting the plate with a jar filled with water. Do not use a can as the salt water would corrode it. Leave for 24 hours.

Drain the onions, remove their skins and return them to the clean bowl. Make up a fresh solution of brine, using the rest of the salt and a further 2 litres/3½ pints water. Pour it over the onions, weight as before and leave for a further 24 hours.

Drain the onions, rinse them thoroughly to remove excess salt, and drain again. Pack the onions into wide-mouthed jars. Cover with cold spiced vinegar, adding a few mustard seeds to each jar, if liked. Cover with vinegar-proof lids. Label and store in a cool, dark place. Keep for at least 1 month for the flavour to mature before using.

SPICED VINEGAR

You will need 7 g/¼ oz each of the following spices: cloves, allspice berries, cinnamon sticks (broken into short lengths) and fresh root ginger.

Bruise the ginger and place it with the rest of the spices in a clean cloth. Beat lightly to release the flavour, then mix the spices with 1 litre/1¾ pints white or malt vinegar. Pour into a 1.1 litre/2 pint bottle, seal tightly and shake daily for 1 month.

Store in a cool, dry place for at least 1 month more before straining out the spices and returning the vinegar to the clean bottle.

HOME-BAKED BREAD ROLLS

Freeze these bread rolls in advance, then warm them just before serving lunch to fill the kitchen with the appetite-arousing aroma of hot bread.

An informal meal provides the ideal opportunity for catching up with old friends. This easy buffet menu is ideal for small or large gatherings.

Menu for Six or Twelve

DEVILLED HERRING ROES
ANGELS ON HORSEBACK
.....
GOULASH
BUTTERED PASTA
GREEN SALAD
.....
MANGO MOUSSE
PAVLOVA

A thoroughly practical menu leaves the hosts free to join in the conversation without having to dash in and out of the kitchen. Basing the meal on a casserole, with simple accompaniments and cook-ahead desserts, could not be simpler and the menu can be prepared for any number from four to forty. In this case, the basic recipes will all serve six, and quantities can be doubled to serve twelve. As long as you have a casserole that is big enough, the additional work involved will be minimal.

The only dishes that require last-minute attention are the savouries which are served with drinks instead of a starter. Prepare the savoury butter for the Devilled Herring Roes and have the roes ready for cooking at the last minute. Similarly, the oysters should be wrapped in bacon, ready to grill. If you are catering for twelve, ask a friend to help by handing out these savouries as you cook them.

GREEN SALAD

Take full advantage of the wide choice of salad leaves and herbs available today to make a salad that sings with flavour. Shred the leaves finely as juggling frilly leaves on a fork while supporting a plate in the other hand is difficult, and this is often one reason why guests avoid the salad at a buffet. As well as lettuce (Iceberg, Little Gem or Cos), include finely sliced celery, diced peeled cucumber, diced green pepper and chopped spring onions. Watercress and a small amount of peppery rocket will pep up the salad. For a pleasing freshness, add plenty of roughly chopped parsley.

DRESSING STYLE

Toss a straightforward oil and vinegar dressing with the salad at the last minute or place it on the table so that guests may help themselves: in a screw-top jar, shake salt, pepper, 5 ml/1 tsp made mustard and 2.5 ml/½ tsp sugar with 45 ml/3 tbsp vinegar until the sugar has dissolved. (Cider vinegar is mild, balsamic vinegar is rich and full-bodied, while wine vinegar tends to be more tangy or harsh.) Add 150 ml/¼ pint olive oil or a mixture of a salad oil and olive oil, then shake well.

PASTA CHOICE

Pick neat pasta shapes for a buffet as they are easier to eat with a fork than long shapes or strands. Shells, wheels, short twists, horns and ears or caps are suitable. Avoid long ′tubes or twists, noodles and spaghetti. Cook the pasta according to the instructions on the packet, drain it thoroughly and transfer to a serving dish which may be placed in the microwave or stood over a pan of simmering water. Add a generous knob of butter and toss the pasta lightly. Cover the dish and set aside. Reheat the pasta in the microwave or by placing the covered bowl over a saucepan of barely simmering water.

CLARIFIED BUTTER

This is prepared by melting butter in a small saucepan, then heating it gently until the sizzling ceases and a white sediment forms. The butter is then poured into a separate container, sometimes through muslin, leaving the sediment behind.

Devilled Herring Roes

MAKES 6

200 g/7 oz soft herring roes
30 ml/2 tbsp plain flour
salt and pepper
clarified butter (opposite) for shallow frying
50 g/2 oz butter, softened
3 anchovy fillets, mashed
lemon juice
3 slices of bread
cayenne pepper
paprika

Rinse the herring roes. Spread the flour in a shallow bowl, add salt and pepper to taste and roll the herring roes lightly in the seasoned flour until coated.

Melt the clarified butter in a frying pan, add the floured roes and fry for about 10 minutes until golden brown all over. Drain on absorbent kitchen paper.

Mix half the softened butter with the anchovy fillets in a small bowl. Add a dash of lemon juice and a little black pepper to taste. Toast the bread and cut off the crusts. Cut each slice in half and spread with the anchovy butter. Arrange the roes on the buttered toast and place in a heated dish.

Melt the remaining butter in a frying pan until nut brown and foaming. Add a squeeze of lemon juice and a pinch of cayenne. Pour the mixture over the roes, dust with paprika and serve very hot.

Angels on Horseback

MAKES 6

6 large shelled oysters
6 rindless streaky bacon rashers
2 slices of bread
butter for spreading

Wrap each oyster in a bacon rasher. Fasten the rolls with small poultry skewers, place in a grill pan and grill for 4–6 minutes. Meanwhile toast the bread. Spread with butter and cut each slice into three fingers. Remove the skewers and serve the 'angels' on the toast.

Goulash

SERVES 6

675 g/1½ lb chuck or blade steak, trimmed
50 g/2 oz dripping or lard
2 onions, sliced
30 ml/2 tbsp plain flour
125 ml/4 fl oz beef stock
125 ml/4 fl oz red wine
450 g/1 lb tomatoes, peeled and diced or 1 (397 g/14 oz)
can chopped tomatoes
2.5 ml/½ tsp salt
15 ml/1 tbsp paprika
1 bouquet garni
450 g/1 lb potatoes
150 ml/¼ pint soured cream

Cut the steak into 2 cm/¾ inch cubes. Heat the dripping in a flameproof casserole and fry the meat until browned on all sides. Using a slotted spoon, remove the meat and set aside. Add the onions to the fat remaining in the casserole and fry gently until just beginning to brown.

Add the flour and cook, stirring, until browned. Gradually add the stock and wine, with the tomatoes, salt, paprika and bouquet garni. Bring to the boil, stirring, then lower the heat and simmer for 1–2 hours or until the meat is tender. Alternatively, transfer the goulash to a casserole and bake in a preheated oven at 160°C/325°F/gas 3 for 1–2 hours.

Thirty minutes before the end of the cooking time, peel the potatoes, cut them into cubes and add them to the goulash. When cooked they should be tender but not broken. Just before serving, remove the bouquet garni and stir in the soured cream.

Mango Mousse

SERVES 6-8

1 kg/2¼ lb ripe mangoes
90 ml/6 tbsp fresh lime juice
100 g/3½ oz caster sugar
15 ml/1 tbsp gelatine
2 egg whites
pinch of salt
100 ml/3½ fl oz double cream
15 ml/1 tbsp light rum

Peel the fruit and cut the flesh off the stones. Purée with the lime juice in a blender or food processor. When smooth, blend in the sugar, then scrape the mixture into a bowl with a spatula. Alternatively, rub the mango through a sieve into a bowl, then stir in the lime juice and sugar.

Place 45 ml/3 tbsp water in a small bowl. Sprinkle the gelatine on to the liquid. Set aside for 15 minutes until the gelatine is spongy, then stand the bowl over a pan of hot water and stir until the gelatine has dissolved completely. Cool slightly, then stir into the mango purée.

In a clean, grease-free bowl, whisk the egg whites with the salt until they form fairly stiff peaks. Stir 15 ml/1 tbsp of the egg whites into the purée to lighten it, then fold in the rest. Lightly whip the cream and rum together in a separate bowl, then fold into the mango mixture as lightly as possible. Spoon into a serving bowl. Refrigerate for about 3 hours until set.

Pavlova

SERVES 6-8

3 egg whites
150 g/5 oz caster sugar
2.5 ml/½ tsp vinegar
2.5 ml/½ tsp natural vanilla essence
10 ml/2 tsp cornflour
FILLING
250 ml/8 fl oz double cream
caster sugar (see method)
2 peaches, skinned and diced
2 kiwi fruit, peeled, sliced and halved
175 g/6 oz seedless grapes

Line a baking sheet with non-stick baking parchment. Draw a 20 cm/8 inch circle on the paper. Set the oven at 150°C/300°F/gas 2.

In a large bowl, whisk the egg whites until stiff and dry. Continue whisking, gradually adding the sugar until the mixture stands in stiff, glossy peaks. Beat in the vinegar, vanilla and cornflour.

Spread the meringue over the circle, piling it up at the edges to form a rim, or pipe the circle and rim from a piping bag fitted with a large star nozzle.

Bake for about 1 hour or until the pavlova is crisp on the outside and has the texture of marshmallow inside. It should be pale coffee in colour. Leave to cool, then carefully remove the pavlova from the baking parchment and put it on a large serving plate.

Make the filling by whipping the cream in a bowl with caster sugar to taste. Lightly fold in the peaches and pile the mixture into the cold pavlova shell. Decorate with kiwi fruit and grapes and serve as soon as possible.

PEELING PEACHES

Place the peaches in a bowl and pour in freshly boiling water to cover them. Leave the peaches to stand for about 1 minute – tender ripe fruit will be ready in about 30 seconds while very firm fruit needs 1–1½ minutes to loosen the peel.

Drain the peaches and, handling them carefully, use the point of a knife to slit the peel which will slide off the fruit easily once cut.

DEVILLED HERRING ROES AND ANGELS ON HORSEBACK

Make more of a simple hot buffet by offering these delicious hot snacks to guests as they arrive.

Cook-Ahead Cold Buffet

> *D*ecorate the buffet table in flamboyant style, with swags of greenery and ribbon bows around the sides, and an arrangement of flowers. Light the table with tapered candles for an evening meal.

Menu for Twelve

CREAMED SALMON IN PASTRY
BAKED HAM
POTATO SALAD (PAGE 41)
MRS BEETON'S WINTER SALAD
GREEN SALAD (PAGE 32)
TOMATO SALAD
.....
SACHER TORTE
PEARS IN RED WINE
.....
CHEESEBOARD

Prepare two quantities of the recipes where indicated, one large bowl of green salad (based on a large Iceberg) and a tomato salad consisting of 24 tomatoes. A baked ham weighing 1.8–2.25 kg/4–5 lb will provide sufficient portions. French bread should be available, sliced fairly thinly, and you will need a basket of biscuits for the cheese: water biscuits and oatcakes are a better choice than salty or strongly flavoured crackers.

For the cheeseboard, choose traditional British cheeses, including a Cheddar or white cheese, such as Wensleydale, a blue cheese, such as Stilton or Blue Cheshire and a more unusual variety, such as Hereford Hop, a mild, buttery cheese coated in hops. If you prefer an international selection, include a semi-soft brie (or similar cheese) and a strong, creamy blue cheese of the Roquefort type. A practical alternative if you have a good local cheese specialist, or a reliable delicatessen at your local supermarket, is to buy a small whole brie or a half or whole Stilton. Order the cheese in advance, asking the supplier to ensure that it is ripe, so that you can be confident that it is of good quality and ready for eating.

BAKED HAM

Larger supermarkets, delicatessens and some butchers will provide whole cooked hams or cooked joints of good-quality ham. The ham may be finished by removing the rind (if this has not already been done), coating the fat with a generous sprinkling of soft light brown sugar, then baking the joint in a preheated oven at 200°C/400°F/gas 6 for about 20 minutes until the sugar has caramelized.

To cook a fresh ham, boil it with sliced onion, carrot, celery and a bouquet garni, allowing 20 minutes per 450 g/1 lb plus 20 minutes. Then remove the skin, coat the fat with sugar and brown it in the oven as above. The ham may be served hot, or cold as here.

PEELING TOMATOES

Peeled tomatoes make the best salads – the result repays the effort. Place the tomatoes in batches of no more than 12 in a large bowl and pour in boiling water from a kettle to cover them. Leave deep-red ripe tomatoes for about 30 seconds, and very firm tomatoes for 1 minute. Drain the tomatoes and slit the peel with the point of a sharp knife; it should rub off easily.

Creamed Salmon in Pastry

Make two of these salmon-filled pastry envelopes if serving 12. They are excellent as part of a cold buffet, but also taste good hot.

SERVES 6

125 ml/4 fl oz white wine
1 bouquet garni
1 onion, sliced
salt and pepper
450 g/1 lb salmon pieces or steaks
50 g/2 oz butter
25 g/1 oz plain flour
150 g/5 oz mushrooms, sliced
75 ml/5 tbsp double cream
450 g/1 lb puff pastry, thawed if frozen
plain flour for rolling out
beaten egg for glazing
GARNISH
lemon wedges
dill sprigs

Put the wine in a small saucepan with 125 ml/4 fl oz water. Add the bouquet garni and onion slices, with salt and pepper to taste. Bring to the boil, lower the heat and simmer for 5 minutes. Strain into a clean pan, add the salmon and poach gently for 10–15 minutes or until cooked. Using a slotted spoon, transfer the fish to a board. Remove the skin and any bones; flake the flesh. Reserve the cooking liquid.

Melt half the butter in a saucepan. Stir in the flour and cook over low heat for 2–3 minutes, without allowing the mixture to colour. Gradually add the reserved cooking liquid, stirring constantly until the sauce boils and thickens. Lower the heat and simmer for 3–4 minutes. Stir in the flaked salmon and remove from the heat.

Melt the remaining butter in a frying pan. Add the mushrooms and fry for 3–4 minutes. Using a slotted spoon, add the mushrooms to the salmon mixture. Stir in the cream, cover the surface of the mixture with damp greaseproof paper and set aside.

Set the oven at 200°C/400°F/gas 6. Roll out the pastry to a thickness of 3 mm/⅛ inch on a floured surface. Cut to a 25 cm/10 inch square, reserving the pastry trimmings. Place the salmon mixture in the centre and brush the edges of the pastry with beaten egg. Lift the corners of the pastry to the middle, enclosing the filling. Seal with beaten egg. Make leaf shapes from the trimmings and use to hide the seal on the top of the pastry envelope. Glaze with egg.

Place the pastry envelope on a baking sheet and bake for 15 minutes. Lower the temperature to 190°C/375°F/gas 5 and bake for 20 minutes more. Serve cold, garnished with lemon wedges and dill.

Mrs Beeton's Winter Salad

SERVES 12 (AS PART OF A BUFFET)

1 head of endive, washed and shredded
1 punnet of mustard and cress
6 celery sticks, thinly sliced
6 hard-boiled eggs, sliced
450 g/1 lb cooked beetroot, sliced
DRESSING
5 ml/1 tsp French mustard
5 ml/1 tsp caster sugar
60 ml/4 tbsp salad oil
30 ml/2 tbsp cider vinegar
salt
cayenne pepper

Arrange the endive, mustard and cress and celery in a salad bowl. Top with the eggs and beetroot, overlapping the slices or interleaving them with the endive but keeping them separate from each other.

For the dressing, put the mustard and sugar in a small bowl. Gradually add the oil, whisking all the time. Trickle in the vinegar, whisking all the time. Add salt and a hint of cayenne. Spoon this dressing over the salad just before serving.

Sacher Torte

Invented by Franz Sacher, this is one of the most delectable cakes imaginable. Serve it solo, or with whipped cream. The icing owes its gloss to glycerine, which is available from chemists. Do not refrigerate the finished cake as this will spoil the glossy appearance of the icing.

SERVES 12

butter for greasing
175 g/6 oz unsalted butter
175 g/6 oz icing sugar
6 eggs, separated
175 g/6 oz plain chocolate, in squares
2.5 ml/½ tsp natural vanilla essence
150 g/5 oz plain flour, sifted
about 125 ml/4 fl oz apricot jam, warmed and sieved, for filling and glazing
ICING
150 g/5 oz plain chocolate, in squares
125 g/4 oz icing sugar, sifted
12.5 ml/2½ tsp glycerine

Line and grease a 20 cm/8 inch loose-bottomed cake tin. Set the oven at 180°C/350°F/gas 4.

In a mixing bowl, beat the butter until creamy. Add 100 g/4 oz of the icing sugar, beating until light and fluffy. Add the egg yolks, one at a time, beating after each addition. Melt the chocolate with 30 ml/2 tbsp water in a heatproof bowl over hot water. Stir into the cake mixture with the vanilla essence.

In a clean, grease-free bowl, whisk the egg whites to soft peaks. Beat in the remaining icing sugar and continue beating until stiff but not dry. Fold into the chocolate mixture alternately with the sifted flour, adding a spoonful of each at a time.

Spoon the mixture into the prepared cake tin and set the tin on a baking sheet. With the back of a spoon, make a slight depression in the centre of the cake to ensure even rising. Bake for 1–1¼ hours or until a metal skewer inserted in the centre of the cake comes out clean.

Leave the cake in the tin for a few minutes, then turn out on to a wire rack. Cool to room temperature.

Split the cake in half and brush the cut sides with warmed apricot jam. Sandwich the layers together again and glaze the top and sides of the cake with apricot jam. Make the icing: melt the chocolate with 75 ml/5 tbsp water in a heatproof bowl over hot water. Stir in the icing sugar and whisk in the glycerine, preferably using a balloon whisk.

Pour the icing over the cake, letting it run down the sides. If necessary, use a metal palette knife, warmed in hot water, to smooth the surface. Avoid touching the icing too much at this stage, or the gloss will be lost. Serve when the icing has set.

Pears in Red Wine

Double the quantities to serve 12.

SERVES 6

175 g/6 oz sugar
45 ml/3 tbsp redcurrant jelly
1 cinnamon stick
6 large ripe cooking pears
350 ml/12 fl oz red wine
40 g/1½ oz flaked almonds

Combine the sugar, redcurrant jelly, and cinnamon stick in a saucepan wide enough to hold all the pears upright so that they fit snugly and will not fall over. Add 350 ml/12 fl oz water and heat gently, stirring, until the sugar and jelly have dissolved.

Peel the pears, leaving the stalks in place. Carefully remove as much of the core as possible without breaking the fruit. Stand the pears upright in the pan, cover, and simmer gently for 15 minutes.

Add the wine and continue to cook, uncovered, for 15 minutes more. Remove the pears carefully with a slotted spoon and arrange them on a serving dish.

Remove the cinnamon stick from the pan and add the almonds. Boil the liquid remaining in the pan rapidly until it is reduced to a thin syrup. Pour the hot syrup over the pears, leave to cool, then chill before serving.

CREAMED SALMON IN PASTRY

Bake fresh salmon in a golden puff-pastry case to create a splendid hot or cold buffet dish without the expense or expertise involved in dressing a whole fish.

Traditional Festive Buffet

Relax on Boxing Day with this gloriously informal but festive spread – a buffet for browsers rather than a set meal. Encourage everyone to help with the preparation, and do not worry if some guests are content with just a plate of ripe cheese and sweet grapes.

Menu for Six

BEEF GALANTINE
BAKED HAM (PAGE 36)
COLD ROAST TURKEY
POTATO SALAD
CELERY AND CHESTNUT SALAD
FENNEL AND CUCUMBER SALAD
.....
MRS BEETON'S TRIFLE
.....
CHEESEBOARD
FRESH FRUIT

Crisp and crunchy salads are a refreshing treat in the round of Christmas feasting, and they go particularly well with cold roast turkey.

The beef galantine can be made and chilled a couple of days in advance. If preferred, baked potatoes or boiled salad potatoes can be served instead of the potato salad.

TURKEY PRESENTATION

For information on roasting turkey see page 48. The leftovers of a roast turkey are not the most attractive sight, but with a little care, yesterday's turkey can look extremely appetizing. Slice all the meat off the carcass, making the breast slices as neat as possible and cutting the nuggets of meat from underneath the bird. Use a sharp, pointed knife to cut away all the meat from the legs and the remaining small areas of brown meat around the thighs.

Arrange the slices so that they overlap neatly, then spoon the chunks and offcuts in neat lines alongside the slices. Neat spoonfuls of stuffing may be arranged around the edge of the platter if there is enough room, but always leave a little space for a garnish. Sliced tomato and cucumber or sprigs of fresh herbs, such as sage and parsley, are ideal.

FOOD SAFETY REMINDER

It is easy to overlook the basic rules of food safety when the house is full of hungry guests and everyone is having far too much fun to be terribly practical.

Remember to cool and chill leftovers as soon as possible. Meat, poultry and other protein foods are particularly vulnerable. Plan ahead to make sure that you will have sufficient space to accommodate the cold cooked turkey in the refrigerator. It is a good idea to sort out the refrigerator just before Christmas, checking the contents, cleaning the shelves and storage areas, and turning the temperature control to a slightly cooler setting to counteract the extra load.

Do not leave leftovers in a warm room for hours after a meal. Clear perishable foods promptly. Carve cold roast meat or poultry off the bone and chill it, then take as much as you require from the refrigerator rather than removing the whole carcass whenever you need enough meat for a sandwich.

Beef Galantine

The browned breadcrumbs and aspic improve the appearance of the galantine but are not essential. A garnish of fresh herb sprigs or salad should be added to the platter along with the aspic (if used).

SERVES 6–8

200 g/7 oz lean rindless back bacon, minced
450 g/1 lb chuck or blade steak, minced
150 g/5 oz fresh white or brown breadcrumbs
salt and pepper
1 egg, beaten
75 ml/3 fl oz beef stock
60 ml/4 tbsp browned breadcrumbs (see below)
margarine or lard for greasing
125 ml/4 fl oz chopped aspic jelly, to garnish (optional)

The galantine may either be steamed or boiled in stock. If the former, prepare a steamer. Alternatively, half fill a large saucepan with stock and bring to the boil.

Combine the bacon, meat and breadcrumbs in a bowl. Add salt and pepper to taste and mix well. Stir the egg and measured stock together and combine this thoroughly with the meat mixture. Shape into a short, thick roll, then wrap in greased greaseproof paper. Wrap in a scalded pudding cloth or foil, tying or twisting the ends securely.

Put the roll on the perforated part of the steamer, curving it round if necessary, and steam for 2 hours, or lower it gently into the fast-boiling stock, lower the heat and simmer for 2 hours. Check the volume of water frequently if using a steamer, and top it up with boiling water from a kettle as necessary.

When cooked, lift out the roll, unwrap it, and then roll it up tightly in a clean dry pudding cloth. Press the roll between two plates until just cold. Then remove the cloth, roll the meat in the breadcrumbs and chill until ready to serve. Place on a plate and garnish with aspic jelly, if liked.

BROWNED BREADCRUMBS
Also known as raspings, these are made by baking bread or crusts in a moderate oven until dry and browned, then crushing them with a rolling pin.

Potato Salad

SERVES 6

salt and pepper
6 large new potatoes or waxy old potatoes
150 ml/¼ pint mayonnaise
3 spring onions, chopped
30 ml/2 tbsp chopped parsley

Bring a saucepan of salted water to the boil, add the potatoes in their jackets and cook for 20–30 minutes until tender. Drain thoroughly. When cool enough to handle, peel and dice the potatoes. Put them in a bowl and add the mayonnaise while still warm. Lightly stir in the spring onions and parsley, with salt and pepper to taste. Cover, leave to become quite cold and stir before serving.

VARIATIONS
French Potato Salad Substitute 100 ml/3½ fl oz French dressing for the mayonnaise. Omit the spring onions, increase the parsley to 45 ml/3 tbsp and add 5 ml/1 tsp chopped fresh mint and about 5 ml/1 tsp snipped chives.

German Potato Salad Omit the mayonnaise and spring onions. Reduce the amount of parsley to 5 ml/1 tsp and add 5 ml/1 tsp finely chopped onion. Heat 60 ml/4 tbsp vegetable stock in a saucepan. Beat in 15 ml/1 tbsp white wine vinegar and 30 ml/2 tbsp oil. Add salt and pepper to taste. Pour over the diced potatoes while still hot and toss lightly. Serve at once, or leave to become quite cold.

Potato Salad with Apple and Celery Follow the basic recipe, but add 2 sliced celery sticks and 1 diced red-skinned apple tossed in a little lemon juice.

Celery and Chestnut Salad

SERVES 6

1 Cos or Iceberg lettuce, shredded
350 g/12 oz cooked chestnuts, halved or quartered
8 celery sticks, finely chopped
2 eating apples
150 ml/¼ pint mayonnaise

Line a salad bowl with the lettuce. Mix the chestnuts and celery in a separate bowl. Peel, core and dice the apples and add them to the celery mixture with the mayonnaise. Mix well, then pile the mixture into the lettuce-lined bowl. Serve at once.

Fennel and Cucumber Salad

SERVES 6

½ large cucumber, diced
6 radishes, sliced
1 fennel bulb, sliced
1 garlic clove, crushed
5 ml/1 tsp chopped mint
2 eggs, hard boiled and quartered, to garnish
DRESSING
30 ml/2 tbsp olive oil
15 ml/1 tbsp lemon juice
salt and pepper

Combine the cucumber, radishes, fennel and garlic in a salad bowl. Sprinkle with the mint. Make the dressing by shaking all the ingredients in a tightly-closed screw-topped jar. Pour over the salad, toss lightly and serve with the hard-boiled egg garnish.

Mrs Beeton's Trifle

Plain whisked or creamed sponge cake, individual buns, or Madeira cake are ideal for this trifle.

SERVES 6

4 slices of plain cake or individual cakes
6 almond macaroons
12 ratafias
175 ml/6 fl oz sherry
30–45 ml/2–3 tbsp brandy
60–90 ml/4–6 tbsp raspberry or strawberry jam
grated rind of ½ lemon
25 g/1 oz flaked almonds
300 ml/½ pint double cream
30 ml/2 tbsp icing sugar
candied and crystallized fruit and peel to decorate
CUSTARD
25 g/1 oz cornflour
25 g/1 oz caster sugar
4 egg yolks
5 ml/1 tsp vanilla essence
600 ml/1 pint milk

Place the sponge cakes in a glass dish. Add the macaroons and ratafias, pressing them down gently. Pour about 50 ml/2 fl oz of the sherry into a bowl and set it aside, then pour the rest over the biscuits and cake. Sprinkle with the brandy. Warm the jam in a small saucepan, then pour it evenly over the trifle base. Top with the lemon rind and almonds.

For the custard, mix the cornflour, caster sugar, egg yolks and vanilla essence to a smooth cream with a little of the milk. Heat the remaining milk until hot. Pour some of the milk on to the egg mixture, stirring, then pour the mixture back into the saucepan with the rest of the milk. Bring to the boil, stirring constantly, then lower the heat and simmer for 3 minutes. Pour the hot custard over the trifle base and cover the surface with dampened greaseproof paper. Set aside to cool.

Add the cream and icing sugar to the reserved sherry and whip until the mixture stands in soft peaks. Swirl the cream over the top of the trifle and chill. Decorate with pieces of candied and crystallized fruit and peel before serving.

MRS BEETON'S TRIFLE

Trifle is guaranteed to be a buffet-party success with adults and children – and this classic recipe is irresistibly luscious.

Roast Beef Dinner

*C*elebrate the best of British cooking with these classic dishes, at one time the weekly favourites in large households, now reserved for high days and holidays when family and friends gather around the groaning table.

When serving a splendid menu of these proportions, the meal should be unhurried, allowing plenty of time for each course to be savoured before the next is served. Do not make the mistake of serving huge portions or the diners will lose their appetites for the pudding and cheese courses.

The soup and Snowdon Pudding can be cooked well in advance and frozen. They should be transferred from the freezer to the refrigerator the day before the meal and allowed to thaw overnight. Before serving, they must be thoroughly reheated. Cover the pudding with greaseproof paper and a double layer of foil and reheat it in a steamer over hot water. Alternatively, stand it in a water bath and reheat it in the oven.

SERVING SMOKED SALMON

Allow about 75 g/3 oz per portion and arrange the slices on individual plates, overlapping or folding them neatly. Add a wedge of lemon to each portion and offer a pepper mill at the table.

Thin bread and butter is the classic, essential accompaniment. White, brown or rye bread are suitable. Remove the crusts and cut each buttered slice across in half to make neat triangles.

YORKSHIRE PUDDING

Yorkshire pudding is traditionally cooked in a large tin below the joint, so that some of the cooking juices from the meat fall into the pudding to give it an excellent flavour. In a modern oven, this means using a rotisserie or resting the meat directly on the oven shelf. About 35–45 minutes before the meat is cooked, remove the roasting pan placed under the joint to catch the drips and spoon off 30 ml/2 tbsp of the dripping into a large baking tin. Place the tin under the joint in the oven for 5 minutes until the fat is very hot, then carefully pour in the batter. Bake until well risen and golden brown. Cut into portions to serve.

WARMING BATH OLIVERS

Plain Bath Oliver biscuits are extremely good served warm with cheese. Take care not to let the crackers get so hot that they cook, but wrap them in foil and place them in a moderate oven for just 3–5 minutes. If the oven has been turned off, the biscuits may be warmed for a longer period in the residual heat. Serve them wrapped in a warm napkin.

Celery Soup

SERVES 6

45 g/1½ oz butter
1 head of celery, finely sliced
3 leeks, trimmed, sliced and washed
1.12 litres/2 pints chicken stock
salt and pepper
grated nutmeg
3 egg yolks
200 ml/7 fl oz single cream

Melt the butter in a large saucepan. Add the celery and leeks and cook gently for 10 minutes until soft.

Add the stock. Bring to the boil, then lower the heat and simmer for 15–20 minutes or until the vegetables are tender. Purée the soup in a blender or food processor, or rub through a sieve into a clean pan. Add salt, pepper and nutmeg to taste. Return the soup to the heat and simmer for 10 minutes.

In a small bowl, mix the egg yolks with the cream. Stir a little of the hot soup into the egg mixture, mix well, then add the contents of the bowl to the soup, stirring over low heat until heated. Do not allow the soup to boil. Serve at once.

FREEZING SOUP

The celery soup – like most other types of soup – can be made in advance and frozen. If freezer space is short, use only half the quantity of stock, then freeze the resulting thick purée. When packing the purée, make a note on the label of the quantity of stock to be added when reheating the soup. Egg yolks and cream curdle when frozen, so do not add them until the soup has been reheated.

Rib of Beef with Yorkshire Pudding

This impressive joint is also known as a standing rib roast. Ask the butcher to trim the thin ends of the bones so that the joint will stand upright. The recipe uses clarified dripping for cooking, but the roast may be cooked without any additional fat.

SERVES 6–8

2.5 kg/5½ lb forerib of beef
50–75 g/2–3 oz beef dripping
100 g/4 oz plain flour
1 egg, beaten
150 ml/¼ pint milk
salt and pepper
vegetable stock or water

Set the oven at 230°C/450°F/gas 8. Wipe the meat but do not salt it. Melt 50 g/2 oz of the dripping in a roasting tin, add the meat and quickly spoon some of the hot fat over it. Roast for 10 minutes.

Lower the oven temperature to 180°C/350°F/gas 4. Baste the meat thoroughly, then continue to roast for a further 1¾ hours for rare meat; 2¼ hours for well-done meat. Baste frequently during cooking.

Meanwhile make the Yorkshire pudding batter: sift the flour into a bowl and add a pinch of salt. Make a well in the centre of the flour and add the beaten egg. Stir in the milk, gradually working in the flour. Beat vigorously until the mixture is smooth and bubbly, then stir in 150 ml/¼ pint water.

About 30 minutes before the end of the cooking time, spoon off 30 ml/2 tbsp of the dripping and divide it between six 7.5 cm/3 inch Yorkshire pudding tins. Place the tins in the oven for 5 minutes or until the fat is very hot, then carefully divide the batter between them. Bake above the meat for 15–20 minutes.

When the beef is cooked, salt it lightly, transfer it to a warmed serving platter and keep hot. Pour off almost all the fat from the roasting tin, leaving the sediment. Pour in enough vegetable stock or water to make a thin gravy, then boil, stirring all the time. Season to taste and serve in a heated gravy boat.

Glazed Carrots

SERVES 6

50 g/2 oz butter
575 g/1¼ lb young carrots, scraped but left whole
3 sugar cubes, crushed
1.25 ml/¼ tsp salt
beef stock (see method)
15 ml/1 tbsp chopped parsley to garnish

Melt the butter in a saucepan. Add the carrots, sugar and salt. Pour in enough stock to half cover the carrots. Cook over gentle heat, without covering the pan, for 15–20 minutes or until the carrots are tender. Shake the pan occasionally to prevent sticking.

Using a slotted spoon, transfer the carrots to a bowl and keep hot. Boil the stock rapidly in the pan until it is reduced to a rich glaze. Return the carrots to the pan, two or three at a time, turning them in the glaze until thoroughly coated. Place on a heated serving dish, garnish with the parsley and serve at once.

WINTER CARROTS
When young carrots are not available, cut large vegetables into wedge-shaped fingers or, if preferred, into fine julienne or matchstick-sized sticks. The carrots can be cut into fancy shapes using a canelle knife (pages 13 and 17).

Snowdon Pudding

Mix the cherries and raisins used in the pudding thoroughly with the dry ingredients before adding the marmalade and liquids. This will prevent the fruit from sinking to the bottom of the pudding.

SERVES 6

fat for greasing
25 g/1 oz glacé cherries, halved
100 g/4 oz raisins
100 g/4 oz dried white breadcrumbs
100 g/4 oz shredded suet
25 g/1 oz ground rice
grated rind of 1 lemon
100 g/4 oz caster sugar
pinch of salt
30 ml/2 tbsp marmalade
2 eggs, beaten
about 75 ml/3 fl oz milk

Grease a 1 litre/1¾ pint pudding basin and decorate the base with some of the cherry halves and raisins. Prepare a steamer or half fill a large saucepan with water. Bring to the boil.

Mix the breadcrumbs, remaining cherries and raisins, suet, ground rice, grated lemon rind, sugar, salt and marmalade in a mixing bowl. Stir in the beaten eggs with enough milk to give a dropping consistency. Spoon the mixture into the prepared basin, cover with greased greaseproof paper and foil and secure with string.

Put the pudding in the perforated part of the steamer, or stand it on an old saucer or plate in the pan of boiling water. The water should come halfway up the sides of the basin. Cover the pan tightly and steam the pudding for 2–2½ hours.

Leave for 5–10 minutes at room temperature to firm up, then turn out on to a serving plate. Serve the pudding with Marmalade and Wine Sauce.

MARMALADE AND WINE SAUCE
Combine 135 ml/9 tbsp orange marmalade and 150 ml/¼ pint dry white wine in a saucepan and heat gently for 5 minutes. Transfer to a jug and serve at once.

SNOWDON PUDDING WITH MARMALADE AND WINE SAUCE

Steaming-hot golden sponge, topped with bright jewel-like fruits, makes this wonderful old-fashioned pudding look as good as it tastes.

*D*eck the table with holly and ivy, arrange Christmas crackers at the place settings and light the festive candles for this most traditional of all family meals.

Menu for Six or Twelve

MELON WITH PARMA HAM
.....
ROAST TURKEY
A SELECTION OF STUFFINGS
ROAST POTATOES
GLAZED CARROTS (PAGE 46)
BRUSSELS SPROUTS WITH
CHESTNUTS
BRAISED CELERY
CRANBERRY SAUCE
BREAD SAUCE
GRAVY
.....
CHRISTMAS PUDDING
RUM OR BRANDY BUTTER
BRANDY SAUCE

The turkey will serve twelve and the other recipes that make up this menu can be doubled to serve the same number, if required. The first course for a filling Christmas dinner should be light and tempting – a brief invitation to the main event.

Prepare the stuffings in advance but do not stuff the bird until Christmas morning. Cranberry sauce and brandy butter should both be prepared on Christmas Eve. Bread sauce and brandy sauce can be made early in the preparation and covered closely with cling film to prevent a skin from forming, then reheated when they are needed, either in the microwave or over gentle heat on the hob.

The Christmas pudding should be put to steam in plenty of time before the meal is served, particularly if hob space is likely to be in demand for cooking vegetables and making gravy.

MELON WITH PARMA HAM

Serve thin slices of peeled melon with fine Parma ham. A honeydew melon will serve six on an occasion like this, when quite modest portions are called for, and 40–50 g/1½–2 oz Parma ham is sufficient per serving. Offer freshly ground black pepper with the starter.

LAYING THE TABLE

Lay the table well in advance, early on Christmas day or the night before if possible when entertaining a crowd as this task can be quite time consuming.

ROASTING TURKEY

Turkey requires long, slow roasting to ensure that the meat is thoroughly cooked. This is particularly important if the body cavity of the bird is stuffed. The following times are for cooking at 180°C/350°F/gas 4. Keep the bird covered with foil until the final 30–45 minutes. These times are a guide only, based upon the bird's weight excluding stuffing, since it is not easy to weigh a stuffed turkey. Birds without stuffing will take slightly less time to cook.

Weight (before stuffing)	Roasting Time at 180°C/350°F/gas 4
2.5 kg/5½ lb	2½ – 3 hours
2.75 – 3.5 kg/6 – 8 lb	3 – 3¾ hours
3.5 – 4..5 kg/8 – 10 lb	3¾ – 4½ hours
4.5 – 5.5 kg/10 – 12 lb	4½ – 5 hours
5.5 – 11.4 kg/12 – 25 lb	20 minutes per 450 g/1 lb plus 20 minutes

Roast Turkey

SERVES 14–16

1 (4.5–5.5 kg/10–12 lb) turkey
salt and pepper
225 g/8 oz rindless streaky bacon rashers
CHESTNUT STUFFING
1 kg/2¼ lb chestnuts
275 ml/9 fl oz turkey or chicken stock
50 g/2 oz butter
1 egg, beaten
single cream or milk (see method)
FORCEMEAT
100 g/4 oz gammon or rindless bacon, finely chopped
50 g/2 oz shredded beef suet
grated rind of 1 lemon
5 ml/1 tsp chopped parsley
5 ml/1 tsp chopped mixed herbs
salt and cayenne pepper
pinch of ground mace
150 g/5 oz fresh white breadcrumbs
2 eggs, lightly beaten

Make the chestnut stuffing first. Make a small slit in the shell of each chestnut, then place the nuts in a saucepan of boiling water. Cook for 5 minutes. Drain carefully and remove the shells and skins while the chestnuts are still hot. Transfer the chestnuts to a clean pan, add the stock and simmer for 20 minutes or until tender. Drain the chestnuts and chop them finely, or press through a sieve into a clean bowl. Melt the butter in a small saucepan. Add to the bowl containing the chestnuts. Stir in the beaten egg, with enough cream or milk to moisten the mixture.

Make the forcemeat. Combine the gammon or bacon, suet, lemon rind and herbs in a bowl. Add salt, cayenne and mace to taste, mix well with a fork, then stir in the breadcrumbs. Gradually add enough beaten egg to bind.

Set the oven at 180°C/350°F/gas 4. Trim the turkey and wash it inside and out in cold water. Pat dry with absorbent kitchen paper and season inside with salt and pepper. Immediately before cooking, fill the neck end of the bird with chestnut stuffing and the body with the forcemeat. Truss if wished, and cover the bird

with the bacon. Place the bird in a roasting tin and roast for 4½–5 hours or until cooked through, removing the bacon towards the end to allow the breast to brown. Serve with gravy.

FORCEMEAT BALLS

If you prefer not to stuff the body cavity of the turkey, make forcemeat balls instead: roll the mixture into 6–8 small balls. Either cook the forcemeat balls around the bird, or fry them in a little oil until browned and cooked through.

Sage and Onion Stuffing

Use this instead of the Chestnut Stuffing or Forcemeat to stuff the turkey; the forcemeat can be shaped into balls and cooked around the bird.

2 onions, thickly sliced
4 young fresh sage sprigs or 10 ml/2 tsp dried sage
100 g/4 oz fresh white breadcrumbs
50 g/2 oz butter, melted
salt and pepper

Put the onions in a small saucepan with water to cover. Bring to the boil, cook for 2–3 minutes, then drain thoroughly. Chop the onions finely. If using fresh sage, chop the leaves finely, discarding any stalk.

Combine the breadcrumbs, onions and sage in a bowl. Add the melted butter, with salt and pepper to taste. Mix well.

Brussels Sprouts with Chestnuts

This is a classic accompaniment for the Christmas turkey. The slightly sweet flavour of the chestnuts is the perfect foil for the Brussels sprouts.

SERVES 6

225 g/8 oz chestnuts, shelled (see below)
1 kg/2¼ lb Brussels sprouts
75 g/3 oz cooked ham, finely chopped
60 ml/4 tbsp single cream
salt and pepper

Set the oven at 180°C/350°F/gas 4. Place the shelled nuts in a saucepan, just cover with water and bring to the boil. Cover the pan, lower the heat, and simmer for about 20 minutes or until the nuts are tender. Drain, then cut each chestnut into quarters.

Trim the sprouts, pulling off any damaged leaves. Using a sharp knife, cut a cross in the base of each. Cook the sprouts in a saucepan of salted boiling water for 5–10 minutes until just tender. Drain well.

Combine the sprouts, chestnuts and ham in a small casserole. Stir in the cream and season with salt and pepper. Cover and bake for 15 minutes.

SHELLING CHESTNUTS

To shell chestnuts, make a small slit in the shell of each, then place the nuts in a saucepan of boiling water. Cook for 5 minutes. Drain, then carefully remove the shells and skins while the chestnuts are still hot.

If you have a microwave the process is even easier: make a slit in the shell of each nut, rinse them thoroughly, but do not dry them. Put the damp nuts in a bowl, cover loosely and cook on High for 5 minutes. When cool enough to handle, remove the shells.

Braised Celery

SERVES 6

25 g/1 oz dripping or butter
3 rindless bacon rashers, chopped
2 onions, finely chopped
1 carrot, finely chopped
½ turnip, finely chopped
chicken stock (see method)
6 celery hearts, washed but left whole
30 ml/2 tbsp chopped fresh parsley

Melt the dripping or butter in a large heavy-bottomed saucepan. Add the bacon and fry for 2 minutes, then stir in the onions, carrot and turnip. Cook over gentle heat, stirring occasionally, for 10 minutes.

Pour over enough chicken stock to half cover the vegetables. Place the celery on top and spoon over some of the stock. Cover the pan tightly with foil and a lid and cook over very gentle heat for 1½ hours or until the celery is very tender. Baste the celery occasionally with the stock.

Using a slotted spoon, transfer the celery to a heated serving dish. Drain the cooking liquid into a small pan, reserving the chopped vegetables.

Boil the cooking liquid rapidly until it is reduced to a thin glaze, then replace the vegetables and pour it over the celery. Sprinkle with the parsley and serve.

Cranberry Sauce

For a festive effect, serve individual portions of bright cranberry sauce in satsuma cups and garnish each with a bay leaf.

MAKES ABOUT 300 ML/½ PINT

150 g/5 oz sugar
225 g/8 oz cranberries

Put the sugar in a heavy-bottomed saucepan. Add 125 ml/4 fl oz water. Stir over gentle heat until the sugar dissolves. Add the cranberries and cook gently for about 10 minutes until they have burst and are quite tender. Spoon into a bowl and leave to cool.

Gravy

SERVES 4–6

**giblets, carcass bones or trimmings from meat,
poultry or game
1 bay leaf
1 thyme sprig
1 clove
6 black peppercorns
¼ onion, sliced
pan juices from roasting
25 g/1 oz plain flour (optional)
salt and pepper**

Place the giblets, bones, carcass and/or trimmings (for example wing ends) in a saucepan. Pour in water to cover, then add the bay leaf, thyme, clove, peppercorns and onion. Bring to the boil and skim off any scum, then lower the heat, cover the pan and simmer for about 1 hour.

Strain the stock and measure it. You need 750 ml/1¼ pints to make gravy for up to six servings. If necessary, pour the stock back into the saucepan and boil until reduced. Pour off most of the fat from the roasting tin, leaving all the cooking juices.

Place the tin over moderate heat; add the flour if the gravy is to be thickened. Cook the flour, stirring all the time and scraping all the sediment off the base of the tin, for about 3 minutes, until it is browned. If the gravy is not thickened, pour in about 300 ml/½ pint of the stock and boil, stirring and scraping, until the sediment on the base of the tin is incorporated.

Slowly pour in the stock (or the remaining stock, if making thin gravy), stirring. Boil for 2–3 minutes, check the seasoning and serve in a gravy boat.

GRAVY NOTES

• The quality of the sediment on the base of the cooking tin determines the quality of the gravy. If the turkey was well seasoned and roasted until well browned outside, the sediment should have a good colour and flavour. Any herbs (other than large stalks), onions or flavouring roasted under the meat should be left in the pan until the gravy is boiled, then strained out before serving.

• Gravy browning may be added; however, it can make the sauce look artificially dark. Pale gravy is perfectly acceptable, provided it has good flavour.

• Always taste gravy when cooked. It should be well seasoned. If it lacks flavour, or is rather dull, a dash of Worcestershire sauce, mushroom ketchup or about 5–15 ml/1–3 tsp tomato purée may be whisked in.

Bread Sauce

MAKES ABOUT 900 ML/1½ PINTS

**600 ml/1 pint milk
1 large onion, studded with 6 cloves
1 blade of mace
4 peppercorns
1 allspice berry
1 bay leaf
100 g/4 oz fine fresh white breadcrumbs
15 ml/1 tbsp butter
salt and pepper
freshly grated nutmeg
30 ml/2 tbsp single cream (optional)**

Put the milk in a small saucepan with the studded onion, mace, peppercorns, allspice and bay leaf. Bring very slowly to boiling point, then remove from the heat, cover the pan and set it aside for 30 minutes.

Strain the flavoured milk into a heatproof bowl, pressing the onion against the strainer to extract as much of the liquid as possible. Stir in the breadcrumbs and butter, with salt, pepper and nutmeg to taste.

Set the bowl over simmering water and cook for 20 minutes, stirring occasionally until thick and creamy. Stir in the cream, if using, just before serving the sauce.

USING THE MICROWAVE FOR MAKING BREAD SAUCE

There is no need to infuse the onion in the milk. Simply put the clove-studded onion in a deep bowl, cover and cook on High for 2 minutes. Add the spices, bay leaf and milk, cover loosely and cook on High for 6–6½ minutes. Stir in the remaining ingredients, except the cream, and cook for 2 minutes more. Remove the studded onion, whole spices and bay leaf. Whisk the sauce, adding the cream if liked.

Christmas Pudding

fat for greasing
225 g/8 oz plain flour
pinch of salt
5 ml/1 tsp ground ginger
5 ml/1 tsp mixed spice
5 ml/1 tsp grated nutmeg
50 g/2 oz blanched almonds, chopped
400 g/14 oz soft dark brown sugar
225 g/8 oz shredded suet
225 g/8 oz sultanas
225 g/8 oz currants
200 g/7 oz seedless raisins
175 g/6 oz cut mixed peel
175 g/6 oz dried white breadcrumbs
6 eggs
75 ml/5 tbsp stout
juice of 1 orange
50 ml/2 fl oz brandy
125–250 ml/4–8 fl oz milk

Grease four 600 ml/1 pint pudding basins. Three-quarters fill four saucepans, each deep enough to hold a single pudding, with water.

Sift the flour, salt, ginger, mixed spice and nutmeg into a very large mixing bowl. Add the almonds, sugar, suet, dried fruit, peel and breadcrumbs.

In a second bowl, combine the eggs, stout, orange juice, brandy and 125 ml/4 fl oz milk. Mix well. Stir the liquid mixture into the dry ingredients, adding more milk if necessary to give a soft dropping consistency.

Divide the mixture between the pudding basins, covering each with greased greaseproof paper and a floured cloth or foil. Secure with string.

Carefully lower the basins into the pans of boiling water. Cover the pans and lower the heat so that the water is kept at a steady simmer. Cook the puddings for 6–7 hours, topping up each pan with boiling water as required. The pudding basins should be covered at all times with boiling water.

To store, cover each pudding with a clean dry cloth, wrap in greaseproof paper and place in an airtight container or seal in a polythene bag. Foil may be used as an outer covering, over paper, but it should not come in direct contact with the pudding or the fruit acid will cause it to break down and disintegrate to a coarse foil powder which will ruin the surface of the pudding. Kept in a cool dry place, Christmas pudding will remain excellent for up to a year. Feed it occasionally with a little brandy.

To reheat, boil or steam each pudding for 1–2 hours. Serve with Rum or Brandy Butter, or Brandy Sauce.

COOKING A CHRISTMAS PUDDING IN A PRESSURE COOKER

Pour 1.5 litres/2¾ pints boiling water into the pressure cooker. Stand the pudding on the trivet and steam it, without weights, for 20 minutes. Bring to 15 lb pressure and cook for 1¾ hours. Allow the pressure to reduce slowly. To reheat, cook at 15 lb pressure for 20 minutes, reduce the pressure slowly and serve.

Brandy Sauce

MAKES ABOUT 900 ML/1½ PINTS

45 ml/3 tbsp cornflour
750 ml/1¼ pints milk
45–60 ml/3–4 tbsp sugar
125 ml/4 fl oz brandy

Put the cornflour in a bowl. Stir in enough of the cold milk to form a smooth, thin paste. Heat the remaining milk in a small saucepan. When it boils, stir it into the cornflour paste, then return the mixture to the clean pan and stir until boiling. Lower the heat and cook, stirring frequently, for 3 minutes. Add sugar to taste and stir in the brandy. Serve hot.

RUM OR BRANDY BUTTER

To make brandy butter, cream 75 g/3 oz unsalted butter until soft, then gradually beat in 175 g/6 oz caster sugar and continue to beat until the mixture is pale and smooth. Adds 30–45 ml/2–3 tbsp rum or brandy a little at a time, beating well after each addition. Chill the butter before serving.

ROAST TURKEY WITH ALL THE TRIMMINGS

The pleasures of the Christmas table – a traditional roast turkey is still the favourite choice in many households.

> *If three days of turkey are not entirely to your taste, sample the alternative delights of roast goose with a rich fruit stuffing and bring the meal to a refreshing end with Mrs Beeton's orange salad which is well laced with Christmas spice.*

Menu for Six

AVOCADO WITH WALNUT OIL
DRESSING
THIN BREAD AND BUTTER
.....
ROAST GOOSE WITH PRUNE
AND APPLE STUFFING
ROAST OR BOILED POTATOES
BRAISED RED CABBAGE
FRENCH BEANS
CREAMED PARSNIPS
.....
MRS BEETON'S ORANGE SALAD
MINCE PIES WITH CANDIED
GINGER CREAM

Goose has rich, dark breast meat which is excellent with a fruit-based stuffing. Unlike turkey, a goose renders a large quantity of fat during cooking and yields a comparatively small amount of meat, so do not count on having leftovers for Boxing Day when serving this menu. Cook the red cabbage in a flameproof casserole at the bottom of the oven.

Mrs Beeton's Orange Salad needs to macerate for 24 hours, so remember to make it early. The result is absolutely worth the wait as the combination of brandy and spice transform the familiar fruit into an astoundingly delicious dessert. As long as the oranges are well moistened with juices, and the container covered tightly, they can be chilled for up to 2 days before the meal.

ADAPTING THE MENU FOR TWO

The stuffing, accompaniments and desserts can be adapted to make a splendid meal for two by roasting a duck instead of the goose. An average duck (about 1.8 kg/4 lb in weight) will give two or three generous portions.

CREAMED PARSNIPS

These can be prepared early on the day of the meal and reheated successfully in the microwave. Peel, slice and cook the parsnips in boiling salted water for 10–20 minutes, depending on the size of the slices. Drain and mash the parsnips, then beat in a good knob of butter and a little single or double cream. Season the parsnips lightly with grated nutmeg.

CANDIED GINGER CREAM

Instead of serving the usual brandy butter with mince pies, stir some chopped candied ginger into whipped double cream. Allow 50–100 g/2–4 oz candied ginger to 300 ml/½ pint cream, depending on how much you like the taste of ginger. Chopped candied ginger is sold prepared, usually alongside baking ingredients such as chopped candied peel.

Avocado with Walnut Oil Dressing

A slightly tangy dressing with crisp, fresh-flavoured vegetables, turns creamy avocado into a lively first course which is not too rich to be served before roast goose. It is important to use a wine vinegar (not a less-tangy cider vinegar) and there are many from which to choose – try light lambrusco vinegar, sharp Champagne vinegar or full-flavoured, slightly darker sherry vinegar.

SERVES 6

2.5 ml/½ tsp sugar
30 ml/2 tbsp white wine vinegar
salt and pepper
30 ml/2 tbsp sunflower oil
60 ml/4 tbsp walnut oil
1 spring onion, finely chopped
1 celery stick, finely chopped
1 small red pepper, seeded and finely chopped
12 lollo rosso leaves, shredded
3 avocados

Whisk the sugar, wine vinegar, salt and pepper together in a bowl until the sugar dissolves. Whisk in the sunflower and walnut oils. Add the spring onion, celery and pepper, stir well and cover the bowl. Leave this dressing to marinate for at least 1 hour before serving.

Divide the lollo rosso between six plates. Halve and stone the avocados. Cut each avocado half lengthways in half again; peel off the skin. Slice the peeled avocado and arrange the slices on the lollo rosso on the plates.

Stir the dressing well to combine the oil and vinegar, then spoon it over the avocados. Serve at once.

Roast Goose with Prune and Apple Stuffing

SERVES 6–8

1 goose with giblets
½ lemon
salt and pepper
350 g/12 oz prunes, soaked overnight in water to cover
450 g/1 lb cooking apples
15 ml/1 tbsp redcurrant jelly

Remove the giblets from the goose and put them in a saucepan. Add 1.5 litres/2¾ pints water and bring to the boil. Lower the heat and simmer until the liquid is reduced by half. Strain and set aside.

Set the oven at 230°C/450°F/gas 8. Weigh the goose and calculate the cooking time at 20 minutes per 450 g/1 lb. Remove the excess fat usually found around the vent. Rinse the inside of the bird, then rub the skin with lemon. Season with salt and pepper.

Drain the prunes, remove the stones and roughly chop the flesh. Put it in a bowl. Peel, core and chop the apples. Add them to the prunes, with salt and pepper to taste. Use the mixture to stuff the body of the bird. Put the goose on a rack in a roasting tin. Place in the oven, immediately lower the temperature to 180°C/350°F/gas 4 and cook for the calculated time. Drain away fat from the roasting tin occasionally during cooking.

When the goose is cooked, transfer it to a heated serving platter and keep hot. Drain off the excess fat from the roasting tin, retaining the juices. Stir in the reserved giblet stock and cook over fairly high heat until reduced to a thin gravy. Stir in the redcurrant jelly until melted. Serve the gravy separately.

Braised Red Cabbage

SERVES 6

50 g/2 oz butter
1.5 kg/3¼ lb red cabbage, finely shredded
50 g/2 oz demerara sugar
75 ml/5 tbsp malt or cider vinegar
salt and pepper

Set the oven at 180°C/350°F/gas 4. Melt the butter in a large flameproof casserole, add the red cabbage and sugar and stir well. Pour in 75 ml/5 tbsp water and the vinegar, with salt and pepper to taste. Cover and cook for about 2 hours, stirring occasionally.

Mrs Beeton's Orange Salad

SERVES 6

8 oranges
75 g/3 oz caster sugar (or to taste)
3.75 ml/¾ tsp ground mixed spice
175 g/6 oz raisins
90 ml/6 tbsp brandy

Peel six of the oranges, removing all the pith. Slice them, discarding the pips. Mix the sugar and spice in a bowl. Layer the orange slices in a serving dish, sprinkling each layer with the sugar mixture and raisins.

Squeeze the juice from the remaining oranges and sprinkle it over the salad. Pour the brandy over, cover and leave to macerate for 24 hours before serving.

Mince Pies

MAKES 12

350 g/12 oz mincemeat
25 g/1 oz icing or caster sugar for dredging
SHORT CRUST PASTRY
300 g/10 oz plain flour
5 ml/1 tsp salt
150 g/5 oz margarine (or half butter, half lard)
flour for rolling out

Set the oven at 200°C/400°F/gas 6. To make the pastry, sift the flour and salt into a bowl, then rub in the margarine until the mixture resembles fine breadcrumbs. Add enough cold water to make a stiff dough. Press the dough together with your fingertips.

Roll out the pastry on a lightly floured surface and use just over half of it to line twelve patty tins. Cut out 12 lids from the rest of the pastry. If liked, make holly leaf decorations from the pastry trimmings.

Place a spoonful of mincemeat in each pastry case. Dampen the edges of the cases and cover with the pastry lids. Seal the edges well. Brush the tops with water and add any pastry decorations. Dredge with the sugar. Make 2 small cuts in the top of each pie. Bake for 15–20 minutes or until golden brown.

RICH SHORT CRUST PASTRY

For melt-in-the-mouth mince pies, make a rich pastry instead of ordinary short crust. Substitute 200 g/7 oz butter for the margarine and bind the pastry with the yolk of 1 large egg instead of water.

ROAST GOOSE WITH PRUNE AND APPLE STUFFING

Crisp and golden roast goose, with its rich dark meat, is the ideal choice for a festive meal for a small family gathering.

Celebration Dinner Party

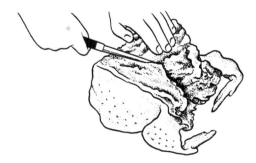

Celebrate in style with this exciting combination of classic dishes – largely prepared in advance – designed to leave the cook confident and relaxed.

Menu for Six

COQUILLES ST JACQUES
MORNAY

.....

GALANTINE OF DUCK
ROAST OR SAUTÉ POTATOES
CAULIFLOWER WITH BEANS
CELERIAC PURÉE

.....

COFFEE MOUSSE
PAVLOVA (PAGE 34)

.....

CHEESEBOARD

Do not let the fact that the galantine requires a boned duck put you off preparing this menu. Given warning, a good butcher will bone the bird, but remember to ask for the bones to be included with the order as they are used for stock. Alternatively, follow this method.

BONING A DUCK

This technique is also used for preparing chicken, pheasant or turkey. There are two key requirements for success, especially if you have never tried boning out a bird before. The first is plenty of time – parts of the technique are fiddly and not to be rushed, particularly when handling a smaller bird, such as pheasant.

A sharp, pointed knife is essential. Ideally a narrow bladed, fine boning knife should be used as it can be manipulated easily around the carcass, but an ordinary, small to medium, cook's knife is quite satisfactory. Additionally, a pair of poultry shears or strong kitchen scissors is useful for snipping flesh and sinew free from joint ends; poultry shears can also be used for cutting through tough joint ends.

Before starting, remember to pay special attention to food hygiene. Yours hands, the surrounding board or work surface and utensils will become slightly messy from contact with the raw poultry, so it is important to wash everything with very hot water using a suitable cleaning agent. It is also a good idea to have hot soapy water ready in the sink for washing your hands without first having to touch the taps.

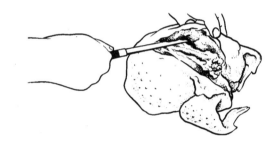

1 *Lay the bird breast down. Cut through the skin and flesh right in to the bone along the length of the back. Beginning at one end of the slit, slide the point of the knife under the flesh and skin.*

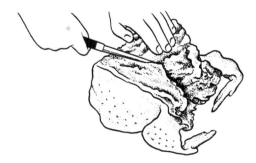

2 *Keeping the knife close to the bone, cut the meat off the bone. Work all the meat off the bone on one side of the carcass, going down the rib cage as far as the breast. Leave the breast meat attached to the soft bone.*

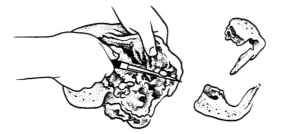

3 *Cut off the wing ends, leaving only the first part of the joint in place. To free the flesh from the wing joint, carefully scrape the meat off the first part, using scissors or the point of the knife to cut sinews.*

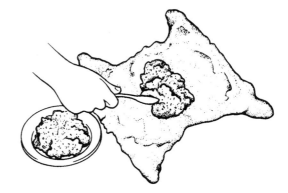

6 *Spread out the boned bird. It is now ready for stuffing.*

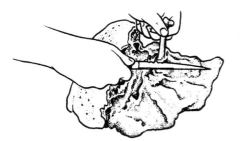

4 *Pull the bones and meat apart as though removing an arm from a sleeve. Again use the point of a knife or scissors to cut sinew and skin attached at the bone end. This leaves the flesh and skin turned inside-out and the bones free but attached to the carcass. Turn the flesh and skin back out the right way. Repeat with the leg.*

Turn the bird and repeat on the second side, again leaving the breast meat attached to the soft bone.

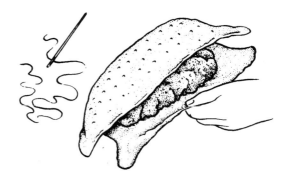

7 *To reshape it, simply fold the sides over the stuffing and sew them with a trussing needle and cooking thread. Turn the bird over with the seam down and plump it up into a neat shape, tucking the boned joint meat under.*

5 *When all the meat has been removed from the second side, and the joints have been boned, the carcass will remain attached along the breast bone. Taking care not to cut the skin, lift the carcass away from the meat and cut along the breast bone, taking the finest sliver of soft bone to avoid damaging the skin.*

Coquilles St Jacques Mornay

These can be prepared up to 24 hours in advance and chilled ready for baking. Great care must be taken not to overcook the scallops. Their delectable flavour and texture is easily spoiled by high heat.

SERVES 6

fat for greasing
675 g/1½ lb potatoes, halved
salt and pepper
75 g/3 oz butter
150 ml/¼ pint single cream
12 large scallops, shelled, with corals
1 small onion, sliced
1 bay leaf
75 ml/5 tbsp dry white wine
juice of ½ lemon
40 g/1½ oz plain flour
200 ml/7 fl oz milk
150 ml/¼ pint single cream
60 ml/4 tbsp dried white breadcrumbs
60 ml/4 tbsp grated Parmesan cheese
watercress sprigs to garnish

Cook the potatoes in a saucepan of salted boiling water for about 30 minutes or until tender. Drain thoroughly and mash with a potato masher, or beat with a hand-held electric whisk until smooth. Beat in 40 g/1½ oz of the butter and 30 ml/2 tbsp of the cream to make a creamy piping consistency.

Grease 6 scallop shells or shallow individual ovenproof dishes. Spoon the creamed potato into a piping bag fitted with a large star nozzle and pipe a border of mashed potato around the edge of each shell. Set the oven at 200°C/400°F/gas 6.

Combine the scallops, onion, bay leaf, wine and lemon juice in a saucepan. Add 125 ml/4 fl oz water. Bring to simmering point and poach the scallops gently for 5 minutes. Using a slotted spoon, remove the scallops and cut them into thick slices. Strain the cooking liquid into a jug.

Melt the remaining butter in a saucepan, add the flour and cook for 1 minute, stirring constantly. Gradually add the reserved cooking liquid, stirring all the time until the sauce starts to thicken. Season to taste and stir in the milk. Bring to the boil, stirring, then lower the heat and simmer for 2–3 minutes. Remove from the heat and stir in the cream.

Divide the sliced scallops between the prepared scallop shells or dishes. Coat with the sauce and sprinkle lightly with the breadcrumbs and Parmesan. Stand the scallop shells or dishes on a large baking sheet and bake for 10 minutes until the breadcrumbs are crisp and the potatoes browned. Garnish with the watercress sprigs and serve at once.

Sauté Potatoes

SERVES 4–6

1.4 kg/3 lb potatoes
salt
25 g/1 oz butter
about 30 ml/2 tbsp oil

Peel the potatoes and cut any large vegetables in half. Cook the potatoes in boiling salted water for 15 minutes, until par-cooked but not completely tender. Drain the potatoes and set them aside to cool in a covered dish.

Cut the potatoes into large chunks. Melt the butter in the oil in a large frying pan and swirl the pan so that both are well mixed. Heat the fat until it is very hot but not smoking and the butter has stopped spitting. Fry the potatoes in the hot fat, turning them frequently after the first few seconds, until they are crisp and golden in places but not completely browned and crusted. Keep the heat under the pan quite high and keep the potatoes moving to prevent them from overbrowning.

Drain the potatoes on absorbent kitchen paper and serve them piping hot.

Galantine of Duck

Given sufficient warning, a good butcher will bone out the duck, but remember to ask for the bones to be included with the order as they are used for the stock. Prepare the duck several hours in advance or the day before, especially if you are boning the bird yourself, and place it in a covered, large dish in the refrigerator.

SERVES 6–8

65 g/2½ oz butter
1 onion, finely chopped
1 garlic clove, crushed
8 juniper berries, crushed
225 g/8 oz chicken livers, chopped
100 g/4 oz rindless streaky bacon rashers, chopped
100 g/4 oz fresh white breadcrumbs
45 ml/3 tbsp chopped parsley
15 ml/1 tbsp finely chopped fresh tarragon
225 g/8 oz cooked ham, chopped
100 g/4 oz no-need-to-presoak dried apricots, chopped
grated rind and juice of 1 orange
salt and pepper
60 ml/4 tbsp port
1 (1.8 kg/4 lb) oven-ready duck, boned
30 ml/2 tbsp oil
300 ml/½ pint red wine
40 g/1½ oz plain flour
STOCK
duck bones
1 unpeeled onion, trimmed, washed and quartered
1 large carrot, thickly sliced
1 celery stick, sliced
1 bay leaf

Melt 25 g/1 oz of the butter in a small saucepan. Add the onion, garlic, juniper berries, chicken livers and bacon. Cook, stirring occasionally, for about 10 minutes, until the livers are firm and the bacon lightly cooked. Stir in the breadcrumbs, parsley, tarragon, ham and apricots. Add the orange rind and seasoning to taste, then bind the mixture with the port.

Set the oven at 190°C/375°F/gas 5. Place the duck bones in a large saucepan with the rest of the ingredients for the stock. Pour in cold water to cover the bones. Bring just to the boil, lower the heat and simmer the stock for 1–1½ hours.

Lay the boned duck flat on a board, skin down, and spread the stuffing over it. Carefully lift the two halves of the duck and bring them together over the stuffing, then sew the skin together using cooking string.

Heat the oil in a roasting tin. Put the duck, breast side up, in the tin and sprinkle generously with salt and pepper. Baste with the hot oil. Transfer to the oven and roast for 1½ hours, basting occasionally with the cooking juices. Pour the orange juice and wine over the duck and cook for a further 30 minutes, until well browned.

Meanwhile, strain the stock and measure 900 ml/ 1½ pints for the sauce. Cream the flour with the remaining butter in a bowl to make a smooth paste or beurre manié.

Transfer the cooked duck to a serving platter, cover with foil and keep the bird hot. Skim any excess fat from the surface of the cooking liquid, then pour in the measured stock. Bring the liquid to the boil, lower the heat slightly and simmer it steadily, scraping the roasting residue off the pan, for 5 minutes. Keeping the sauce at simmering point, gradually whisk in the beurre manié in small lumps, allowing each addition to melt into the sauce before adding the next. When all the beurre manié has been added, bring the sauce to a full boil, reduce the heat slightly to prevent it from boiling over, and cook for 2 minutes. Taste the sauce for seasoning.

Serve the duck carved into thick slices and offer the wine sauce separately. Orange, parsley and fresh tarragon are suitable garnishes for the duck.

COLD GALANTINE OF DUCK
The boned stuffed duck is equally delicious as part of a cold buffet. Do not add the orange juice and wine to the roasting tin. Wrap the cooked duck in foil and leave to cool, then chill it overnight. Glaze the duck with redcurrant jelly, boiled briefly with a little orange juice, and garnish with thin orange slices.

Celeriac Purée

SERVES 4–6

15 ml/1 tbsp lemon juice
1 large celeriac root, about 1 kg/2¼ lb
salt and white pepper
90 ml/6 tbsp single cream
15 ml/1 tbsp butter
60 ml/4 tbsp pine nuts

Have ready a large saucepan of water to which the lemon juice has been added. Peel the celeriac root fairly thickly so that the creamy white flesh is exposed. Cut it into 1 cm/½ inch cubes. Add the cubes to the acidulated water and bring to the boil over moderate heat. Add salt to taste, if required, and cook for 8–10 minutes or until the celeriac is tender.

Drain the celeriac and purée it with the cream and butter in a blender or food processor. Alternatively, mash until smooth, then press through a sieve into a bowl. Reheat the purée if necessary, adjust the seasoning, stir in the nuts and serve at once.

Cauliflower with Beans

SERVES 6

45 ml/3 tbsp oil
1 onion, chopped
1 cauliflower, broken in florets
225 g/8 oz French beans, trimmed and cut in pieces
or thawed and drained if frozen
salt and pepper
15–45 ml/1–3 tbsp chopped fresh herbs

Heat the oil in a large frying pan or wok. Stir fry the onion for 5 minutes, until slightly softened. Add the cauliflower and cook, stirring, for 5 minutes, until the florets are translucent and lightly cooked. Add the beans and continue stir frying for a further 3–4 minutes or until all the vegetables are just cooked but still crunchy. Add salt and pepper to taste and stir in the herbs. Serve.

Coffee Mousse

SERVES 6

350 ml/12 fl oz milk
25 ml/5 tsp instant coffee
3 eggs, separated
75 g/3 oz caster sugar
15 ml/1 tbsp gelatine
100 ml/3½ fl oz double cream
DECORATION
whipped cream
chocolate-coated coffee beans

In a saucepan, warm the milk and stir in the coffee. Set aside. Put the egg yolks into a bowl with the caster sugar and mix well, then gradually add the flavoured milk. Strain through a sieve back into the pan. Stir over very gentle heat for about 10 minutes until the custard starts to thicken. Cool slightly.

Place 45 ml/3 tbsp water in a small bowl and sprinkle the gelatine on to the liquid. Set aside for 15 minutes until the gelatine is spongy. Stand the bowl over a pan of hot water and stir the gelatine until it has dissolved completely. Cool until the gelatine mixture is at the same temperature as the custard, then mix a little of the custard into the gelatine. Stir back into the bowl of custard and leave in a cool place until the mixture is beginning to set.

Whip the cream in a deep bowl until it just holds its shape. In a separate, grease-free bowl, whisk the egg whites until stiff. Fold first the cream, and then the egg whites, into the coffee custard, making sure the mixture is fully blended but not over-mixed.

Pour into six glasses or glass dishes and refrigerate for 1–2 hours until set. Decorate with piped whipped cream and chocolate-coated coffee beans.

COQUILLE ST JACQUES MORNAY

Served in a border of piped mashed potatoes, a first course of scallops in a creamy sauce sets the tone for this elegant menu.

A menu fit for a monarch.
Savour this meal with friends who share your appreciation of the rich flavour of game.

Menu for Six

POTTED VENISON
HOT TOAST FINGERS
.....
GRILLED SALMON STEAKS
SALAD GARNISH
.....
PHEASANT VERONIQUE
LIGHTLY COOKED BROCCOLI
GLAZED CARROTS (PAGE 46)
BOILED POTATOES OR NEW
POTATOES
.....
CHOCOLATE CRUMB PUDDINGS
CHOCOLATE CREAM SAUCE
TROPICAL FRUIT SALAD
(PAGE 26)

Serve this menu with confidence to those who love game, but do check first if you are not sure of your guests' tastes.

The potted venison should be prepared the day before or early on the day and the preparations for the main course should be completed well ahead. The salmon steaks must be served freshly grilled, so preheat the grill while the first course is being eaten, then slip out, telling everyone that you are going to be busy in the kitchen for a few minutes.

Make a crisp, fresh salad garnish to go with the salmon, dressing it just before it is served on individual side plates. Try slightly bitter radicchio, peppery rocket and finely chopped spring onion mixed with small lambs' lettuce leaves or shredded baby spinach leaves and a little shredded Iceberg lettuce. The dressing should be no more than a very simple mixture of oil and vinegar, with salt and freshly ground black pepper added to taste.

Potted Venison

MAKES ABOUT 1 KG/2¼ LB

100–150 g/4–5 oz butter
1 kg/2¼ lb cooked venison, finely minced
60 ml/4 tbsp port or brown stock
1.25 ml/¼ tsp grated nutmeg
1.25 ml/¼ tsp ground allspice
salt
2.5 ml/½ tsp freshly ground black pepper
melted clarified butter (page 32)
hot toast fingers to serve

Melt 100 g/4 oz of the butter in a saucepan. Add the minced venison, port or stock, spices, salt and pepper. If the meat is very dry, add the remaining butter.

Cook the mixture gently until blended and thoroughly hot. Immediately, turn into small pots and leave to cool. Cover with clarified butter. When cool, refrigerate until the butter is firm. Serve with fingers of hot toast.

Grilled Salmon Steaks

Make the maître d'hôtel butter in advance, chill and slice it ready for quickly topping the salmon steaks just before serving them. The butter will keep well in the refrigerator for up to 2 weeks or it may be frozen for up to 3 months.

SERVES 6

50 g/2 oz clarified butter (page 32)
6 small salmon steaks
salt and pepper
6 pats of maître d'hôtel butter (see below), to serve
salad leaves to garnish

Warm the clarified butter in a small saucepan. Sprinkle the salmon steaks with salt and pepper. Brush liberally with the clarified butter. Grill under moderate heat for 4–5 minutes on each side, turning once. Top each portion with a pat of maître d'hôtel butter and add a few salad leaves for a palate-refreshing garnish.

MAÎTRE D'HÔTEL BUTTER

This is made by creaming butter with a little chopped parsley, a good squeeze of lemon juice and a little seasoning. Spoon the butter on to a piece of cling film, then twist it into a cylinder and place in the freezer until firm, or chill for a few hours. Slice into individual pats for serving.

Pheasant Veronique

SERVES 6

3 pheasants
salt and pepper
100 g/4 oz butter
900 ml/1½ pints chicken stock
15 ml/1 tbsp arrowroot
350 g/12 oz seedless white grapes, peeled
90 ml/6 tbsp double cream
5 ml/1 tsp lemon juice

Set the oven at 180°C/350°F/gas 4. Wipe the pheasants, season and rub well all over with butter. Put a knob of butter inside each bird. Place the pheasants, breast side down, in a flameproof casserole. Pour in the stock and cover the birds with buttered paper. Cook for 1–1¼ hours, until tender, turning the birds breast side up after 25 minutes.

Remove the pheasants from the stock and cut into convenient portions for serving; keep hot. Boil the liquid in the casserole to reduce it a little, then strain into a saucepan. Blend the arrowroot with a little water, then stir it into the hot stock. Bring to the boil, stirring, then remove the pan from the heat. Add the grapes, cream and lemon juice, then heat through briefly without boiling. Check the seasoning.

Arrange the pheasants on a serving dish or individual plates, spoon the sauce over and serve.

PHEASANT PORTIONS

Some supermarkets sell pheasant quarters and boneless breast portions. Portions are easier to serve than whole birds, which have to be jointed when cooked.

Substitute six quarters for the whole birds used in the above recipe. Lightly brown the quarters in the butter in a flameproof casserole or frying pan. Transfer the quarters to an ovenproof casserole, if necessary, and season them well. Pour in the stock. Cover the casserole and cook as above, keeping the lid on the casserole throughout the cooking.

Chocolate Crumb Puddings

The mixture is particularly suitable for making individual puddings and the results are so light that they are ideal for 'dressing up' for dinner parties. Simple finishing touches, such as the cream feathered through the sauce, or serving fresh fruit with the puddings, add a note of sophistication.

SERVES 6

fat for greasing
50 g/2 oz plain chocolate
125 ml/4 fl oz milk
40 g/1 oz butter or margarine
40 g/1½ oz caster sugar
2 eggs, separated
100 g/4 oz dried white breadcrumbs
1.25 ml/¼ tsp baking powder
DECORATION
Chocolate Caraque (page 21) or grated chocolate
strawberries, halved (optional)

Grease six dariole moulds. Prepare a steamer over a pan of water and bring to the boil. Grate the chocolate into a saucepan, add the milk and heat slowly to melt the chocolate.

Cream the butter or margarine with the sugar in a mixing bowl. Beat in the egg yolks with the melted chocolate mixture. Add the breadcrumbs and baking powder.

In a clean, grease-free bowl, whisk the egg whites until fairly stiff. Fold them into the pudding mixture. Spoon the mixture into the prepared moulds, cover with greased greaseproof paper and foil, and crumple the edge of the foil on to the rim of the moulds to prevent steam from entering.

Put the puddings in the perforated part of the steamer. Cover and steam the puddings for 30 minutes. Leave the puddings for 3–5 minutes to firm up, then turn out on to serving plates. Serve with the Chocolate Cream Sauce. Top the puddings with chocolate caraque or grated chocolate and decorate with fresh strawberries if liked.

DRIED WHITE BREADCRUMBS

It is important to use dried breadcrumbs in the Chocolate Crumb Puddings as they are finer and absorb more liquid than fresh bread. Spread out fresh breadcrumbs in a roasting tin and place them in the oven until dried but not browned, turning them once or twice. The crumbs may be dried in the residual heat after using the oven for other cooking or the oven should be set to a low temperature to avoid browning the bread.

Crumbs may also be dried in a large bowl in the microwave. Cook on full power for short bursts of 2 minutes, or longer for a large bowlful, stir the crumbs and repeat. When the crumbs feel hot and crisp or dry, allow them to cool before checking their texture: if they are still soft, cook them for another few minutes, cool them and check their texture again.

When cool, reduce the crumbs by processing them in a food processor or blender until fine. Alternatively, the crumbs may be rubbed through a metal sieve. Then weigh the quantity required for the recipe.

Chocolate Cream Sauce

SERVES 6

225 g/8 oz plain chocolate, roughly grated
25 g/1 oz unsalted butter
60 ml/4 tbsp single cream
5 ml/1 tsp natural vanilla essence

Put the grated chocolate in a heatproof bowl with the butter. Add 90 ml/6 tbsp water. Stand the bowl over a saucepan of simmering water and stir until the chocolate and butter have melted.

When the chocolate mixture is smooth, remove from the heat and immediately stir in the cream and vanilla essence. Serve at once.

STYLISH PRESENTATION

Feather a little single cream through the sauce. Put a few drops of cream on to the chocolate sauce, then drag the tip of a cocktail stick through it.

CHOCOLATE CRUMB PUDDINGS WITH CHOCOLATE CREAM SAUCE

Dark and divine – an irresistible chocolate dessert to round off a fabulous celebration of food.

Vegetarian Feast

Menu for Six

Stuffed Mushrooms
Mrs Beeton's Pastry
Ramakins
.....
Melon Fans with Raspberry
Vinegar
.....
Boston Roast
Fresh Tomato Sauce
Cauliflower with Beans
(page 62)
Roasted New Potatoes in
their Skins
.....
Pears in Red Wine
(page 38)
.....
Marzipan Fruits

This lively menu, with its contrasting flavours and textures, will appeal to all who enjoy good food, whether they eat meat or not. The selection of dishes would also tie in with a traditional roast, allowing the first courses, vegetables and dessert to be shared by vegetarians and non-vegetarians alike.

After sampling walnut-stuffed mushrooms and cheese pastries, cleanse the palate with melon and fruity raspberry vinegar. This pair of opening courses would serve equally well as an introduction to roast lamb or pork as they do to a pleasing haricot-bean loaf.

When serving two courses before the main dish, present small amounts of food to arouse the appetite rather than douse it.

MELON FANS WITH RASPBERRY VINEGAR

To cut melon fans, halve a melon and scoop out the seeds. Cut the melon into wedges and remove the peel. Slice each wedge lengthways, three-quarters of the way through, leaving the slices attached at one end. Lay the wedges on serving plates, spreading the slices apart slightly so that they fan out.

Taste some raspberry vinegar and sweeten it, if necessary, so that it has a distinctly sweet-sour flavour. Spoon a little vinegar over each portion of melon, cover and chill well before serving.

COOKING THE BOSTON ROAST AHEAD

The Boston Roast freezes very well. Cool the roast quickly, then wrap it in an airtight polythene bag. Alternatively, the roast may be sliced and the individual slices separated with freezer film before wrapping the re-formed loaf. Separating the slices allows for faster thawing or for individual portions to be thawed as required.

ROASTED NEW POTATOES IN THEIR SKINS

Small new potatoes are delicious roasted in their skins, which become crisp and golden. Cook the potatoes in boiling water for 5 minutes, or until they are part cooked, then drain them and transfer them to a roasting tin. Brush with olive oil or melted butter and place in the oven with the Boston Roast. Turn the potatoes halfway through cooking.

Stuffed Mushrooms

SERVES 6

fat for greasing
12 open cup mushrooms
25 g/1 oz butter
1 garlic clove, crushed
1 onion, finely chopped
50 g/2 oz walnuts, finely chopped
50 g/2 oz fresh white breadcrumbs
30 ml/2 tbsp chopped parsley
salt and pepper

Generously grease an ovenproof dish. Set the oven at 190°C/375°F/gas 5. Clean the mushrooms and remove the stalks. Place the caps in the prepared dish, gills uppermost. Chop the stalks finely.

Melt the butter and fry the mushroom stalks, garlic and onion gently for 5 minutes. Add the walnuts with the breadcrumbs and parsley. Stir in salt and pepper.

Divide the stuffing mixture between the mushroom caps, heaping it up in the centre. Bake the mushrooms for 20–25 minutes, until browned and crisp on top.

Mrs Beeton's Pastry Ramakins

These cheese savouries can be made with the odd pieces of cheese left from a cheeseboard. Mix a little strong cheese with any mild-flavoured leftovers.

MAKES ABOUT 24

oil for greasing
225 g/8 oz puff pastry, thawed if frozen
175 g/6 oz Stilton or Cheshire cheese, or a mixture of Parmesan and mild cheese, grated or finely crumbled
1 egg yolk

Grease a baking sheet. Set the oven at 220°C/425°F/gas 7. Roll out the pastry into an oblong measuring about 20 x 10 cm/8 x 4 inches. Sprinkle half the cheese over the middle of the pastry. Fold the bottom third over the cheese, then fold the top third down. Give the pastry a quarter turn clockwise, then roll it out into an oblong about the same size as the original shape.

Sprinkle the remaining cheese over the pastry and repeat the folding and rolling. Finally, roll out the pastry to about 3 mm/⅛ inch thick, or slightly thicker. Use fancy cutters to stamp out shapes – fluted circles, diamonds, triangles or crescents – and place them on the baking sheet.

Stir 5 ml/1 tsp water into the egg and brush it over the pastries. Bake for 10–15 minutes, until puffed and browned. Serve freshly baked.

Boston Roast

SERVES 6

fat for greasing
300 g/11 oz haricot beans, soaked overnight in cold water to cover
salt and pepper
15 ml/1 tbsp oil
1 onion, chopped
150 g/5 oz Cheddar cheese, grated
60 ml/4 tbsp vegetable stock
1 egg, beaten
100 g/4 oz fresh white breadcrumbs
5 ml/1 tsp dried thyme
2.5 ml/½ tsp grated nutmeg

Drain the beans, put them in a saucepan and add fresh water to cover. Do not add salt. Bring to the boil, cook for 10 minutes, then lower the heat and simmer for about 40 minutes or until tender. Drain the beans. Mash with seasoning or purée in a food processor.

Set the oven at 180°C/350°F/gas 4. Grease a 900 g/ 2 lb loaf tin generously. Heat the oil in a frying pan, add the onion and fry for about 10 minutes, or until softened. Tip the onion into a large bowl and add the mashed or puréed beans with the rest of the ingredients.

Spoon the mixture into the prepared tin. Cover the surface with greased greaseproof paper. Bake for 45 minutes, until firm and slightly shrunk. Serve with Fresh Tomato Sauce (page 70).

Fresh Tomato Sauce

MAKES ABOUT 600 ML/1 PINT

30 ml/2 tbsp olive oil
1 onion, finely chopped
1 garlic clove, crushed
1 bay leaf
1 rindless streaky bacon rasher, chopped
800 g/1¾ lb tomatoes, peeled and chopped
60 ml/4 tbsp stock or red wine
salt and pepper
generous pinch of sugar
**15 ml/1 tbsp snipped fresh basil or 5 ml/1 tsp
dried basil**

Heat the oil in a saucepan and fry the onion, garlic, bay leaf and bacon over gentle heat for 15 minutes.

Stir in all the remaining ingredients except the basil. Heat until bubbling, then cover the pan, lower the heat and simmer gently for 30 minutes or until the tomatoes are reduced to a pulp.

Rub the sauce through a sieve into a clean saucepan or remove the bay leaf and purée in a blender or food processor until smooth, then rub through a sieve to remove seeds, if required. Reheat the sauce. Add the basil and check the seasoning before serving.

FREEZING TOMATO SAUCE

Fresh tomato sauce is an ideal recipe for using up a glut of ripe fruit and it is an invaluable freezer candidate. Season the sauce but do not add the basil before freezing. When cold, pack the sauce in small quantities which will thaw quickly. Plastic cartons are ideal containers, but remember to leave headspace for the sauce to expand slightly as it freezes. Fresh herbs, such as basil or parsley, can be added when the sauce has been reheated.

Marzipan Fruits

Use good-quality white marzipan to make tempting dainties to serve with coffee. Dust your fingers with a little icing sugar while you work. Colour one small piece of marzipan yellow and another green as the two basic colours. Small pieces of these colours can be moulded into the remaining marzipan as required. For best effect, leave the moulded fruits to dry for 24 hours, then paint them with food colouring.

Use cloves to represent the calyx and stalk on fruit. To simulate the rough skin of citrus fruits, use the fine side of a grater. Mould leaves out of marzipan.

Lemon Roll yellow marzipan into a ball and ease out to a soft point at either end. Roll lightly on a fine grater.

Apple Roll green marzipan into a ball, indent the top and use a clove for the stalk. Streak with red food colouring.

Pear Gradually taper a yellow marzipan ball into shape and put a clove in the narrow end for a stalk. Press another clove well into the rounded end for a calyx. Streak with green food colouring.

Banana Shape yellow marzipan into a curved sausage, tapering either end. Colour the tip brown and streak the middle with brown 'ripening' lines, using a brown icing pen or a brush dipped in food colouring.

Orange Use orange-coloured marzipan. Mould into a ball and roll on a fine grater.

Strawberry Shape red marzipan into a ball, then pinch out one end. Paint with red food colouring and sprinkle with caster sugar at once.

Cherries Shape small balls of red marzipan and add long marzipan stalks. These are the ideal shape in which to conceal a hazelnut or raisin.

Peaches Roll peach-coloured marzipan into a ball and indent the top, flattening the paste slightly. Brush with a hint of red food colouring.

BOSTON ROAST AND CAULIFLOWER WITH BEANS

A simple combination of dishes is the main event of a colourful vegetarian four-course meal.

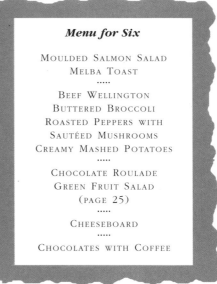

*S*tarch the linen, bring out the best china and polish the silver for this collection of favourite dinner-party dishes, with succulent Beef Wellington as a splendid centrepiece.

Menu for Six

MOULDED SALMON SALAD
MELBA TOAST
.....
BEEF WELLINGTON
BUTTERED BROCCOLI
ROASTED PEPPERS WITH
SAUTÉED MUSHROOMS
CREAMY MASHED POTATOES
.....
CHOCOLATE ROULADE
GREEN FRUIT SALAD
(PAGE 25)
.....
CHEESEBOARD
.....
CHOCOLATES WITH COFFEE

Timing is crucial if you want to serve a perfectly pink Beef Wellington for the main course, but this is not difficult when the menu is carefully planned.

The salmon salad should be prepared the day before, allowing plenty of time for setting the layers. Similarly, do not leave the preparation of the beef until late in the day as the meat does take a while to cool after it has been sealed and before it can be wrapped in pastry. Leaving the beef in pastry overnight in the refrigerator is not a good idea as the juices from the meat seep into the pastry.

MELBA TOAST

Making Melba toast is much easier than it looks, and thin, crisp slices are the perfect accompaniment for pâtés, mousses and aspic savouries. The toast can be prepared some time in advance as it will keep well in an airtight container for several days.

Toast medium-thick slices of white bread on both sides under a hot grill until golden. Working quickly, cut off the crusts and immediately cut horizontally through each slice to separate it into two thin slices. This is simple if the toast is hot, but if it is allowed to cool, and become crisp, the slices will break.

Grill the untoasted sides, placing the bread well away from the heat source so that it does not cook too quickly, but curls and browns lightly without burning. Do not leave the grill unattended. Leave the slices to cool on a wire rack.

ROLLING THE ROULADE

Do not worry too much if cracks appear in the roulade during rolling. The mixture does not include any flour; the baked roulade is rich and sweet but has a fragile texture. Dusting with icing sugar disguises the cracks.

Moulded Salmon Salad

SERVES 6–8

500 ml/17 fl oz fish stock (see below)
25 g/1 oz gelatine
salt and pepper
½ cucumber
2 firm tomatoes, peeled and sliced
225 g/8 oz skinned and boned cooked salmon, flaked

Heat the stock in a saucepan, stir in the gelatine and stir briskly until completely dissolved. Add salt and pepper to taste. Set aside to cool but do not allow to set.

Cover the bottom of a 600 ml/1 pint mould with some cool fish stock. Chill until set. Cut a few thin slices from the cucumber, then peel and thinly slice the rest. Arrange the unpeeled cucumber slices and a few tomato slices on the jelly-lined mould, then pour a little more stock over the top to keep the garnish in place. Chill again until set.

Add a layer of salmon and another layer of stock, and chill again until set. Repeat these layers until the mould is full, then cover and chill until required. Invert the mould on to a platter and serve with crisp Melba toast.

FISH STOCK

To make a superior fish stock for this moulded salad, use white fish trimmings or 225 g/8 oz white fish fillet. Simmer the fish in 150 ml/¼ pint dry white wine and 600 ml/1 pint water with 1 diced carrot, a few parsley stalks, 1 roughly chopped onion and a small stick of celery. Strain the stock after 40 minutes.

For a clear stock, whisk in an egg white and the crushed shell of the egg over medium heat until the egg white forms a frothy crust which begins to rise in the pan. Remove the pan from the heat for a few seconds, then heat the stock again until the stock rises. Repeat once or twice more until the stock is clear, then strain it through a muslin-lined sieve into a clean bowl.

Clarifying is not essential for flavour, but it does give the moulded salad a superior appearance.

Beef Wellington

This classic Beef Wellington differs from beef en croûte in that the meat is covered with fine pâté – preferably pâté de foie gras – before it is wrapped.

SERVES 6

800 g–1 kg/1¾ lb–2¼ lb fillet of beef
freshly ground pepper
25 g/1 oz butter
15 ml/1 tbsp oil
100 g/4 oz button mushrooms, sliced
5 ml/1 tsp chopped fresh mixed herbs
5 ml/1 tsp chopped parsley
450 g/1 lb puff pastry, thawed if frozen
75 g/3 oz fine liver pâté
beaten egg, for glazing

Set the oven at 230°C/450°F/gas 8. Trim the meat and tie it into a neat shape. Season with pepper. Melt the butter in the oil in a large frying pan, add the fillet and brown it quickly all over. Transfer the fillet to a roasting tin, reserving the fat in the pan, and roast it for 10–20 minutes (for rare to medium result). Remove and cool.

Heat the fat remaining in the frying pan, add the mushrooms and fry over moderate heat for 2–3 minutes. Remove from the heat, add the herbs and leave to cool.

Roll out the pastry on a lightly floured surface to a rectangle large enough to enclose the fillet. Using a slotted spoon, transfer the mushroom mixture to one half of the pastry. Lay the beef on top and spread the pâté over the meat. Wrap the pastry around the beef to form a neat parcel, sealing the edges well. Place on a baking sheet with the join underneath. Top with leaves and/or a lattice of strips cut from the pastry trimmings, glaze with beaten egg and bake for about 30 minutes. Serve hot.

INDIVIDUAL BEEF WELLINGTONS

To make individual Beef Wellingtons, use six portions of raw fillet. Wrap individually, including mushrooms and pâté, bringing up the pastry sides to make neat parcels. Glaze and bake, allowing 15–20 minutes for rare beef; 25–30 minutes for medium-cooked beef.

Roasted Peppers with Sautéed Mushrooms

This simple, colourful combination of vegetables provides a refreshing flavour and contrasting texture when served with traditional meat-and-vegetable menus. The peppers are especially delicious with creamy mashed potatoes, and the dish is ideal for using wild mushrooms that are now available from many supermarkets.

3 red or yellow peppers
350 g/12 oz button mushrooms
about 25 g/1 oz butter
about 15 ml/1 tbsp olive oil
salt and pepper

Roast and peel the peppers well in advance: to peel a pepper, skewer it on a metal fork and rotate over the burner on a gas hob until the skin is charred. Alternatively, cook the peppers under a preheated grill, turning them occasionally, until they are blackened on all sides.

Rinse the peppers under cold water and use a small knife to scrape off the skin. Halve the peppers, cut out their cores and all seeds, then rinse them and pat dry on absorbent kitchen paper. Cut the pepper halves across into slices.

Rinse the mushrooms briefly under cold running water. If using wild mushrooms, pick them over thoroughly, trim and rinse them if necessary, then leave them in a colander or sieve.

In a large frying pan or heavy-bottomed saucepan, sauté the peppers for 1 minute in enough butter and olive oil to coat the pan thinly, adding salt and freshly ground black pepper to taste. Add the mushrooms and sauté them for 1–2 minutes, until lightly cooked. Serve the peppers and mushrooms immediately, with the cooking juices poured over.

Chocolate Roulade

SERVES 6

oil and butter for greasing
150 g/5 oz plain dessert chocolate, in squares
4 eggs, separated
100 g/4 oz caster sugar
15 g/½ oz icing sugar, plus extra for dusting
about 175 ml/6 fl oz double cream

Line and grease a 42 x 30 cm/17 x 12 inch Swiss roll tin. Cut out a second sheet of greaseproof paper the same size as that used for lining the tin, to cover the cooked roulade, and have ready a damp clean tea-towel with which to cover the paper-topped roulade. Set the oven at 190°C/375°F/gas 5.

Heat a saucepan of water. Place the chocolate in a heatproof bowl. When the water boils, remove the pan from the heat and set the bowl over it. Leave to melt, stirring occasionally.

Combine the egg yolks and caster sugar in a bowl and beat briskly until the mixture is pale and creamy. Add 45 ml/3 tbsp hot water to the melted chocolate and beat until well blended. Stir the chocolate into the egg yolk mixture, then whisk thoroughly.

In a clean, grease-free bowl, whisk the egg whites until fairly stiff. Using a metal spoon, fold them carefully into the chocolate mixture. Tip into the prepared Swiss roll tin and bake for 20 minutes until the roulade is firm.

Butter the remaining sheet of greaseproof paper. Remove the tin from the oven and immediately cover the cake with the buttered paper and the damp tea-towel. Leave to stand for several hours or overnight.

Next day, remove the cloth. Turn the paper buttered side up, sprinkle with icing sugar and replace sugared side down. Grip the paper and tin and invert both so that the roulade is upside-down. Lay it down on the paper and remove the tin. Peel off the lining paper.

In a bowl, whip the cream until it stands in soft peaks. Spread the cream evenly over the surface of the roulade. Roll the roulade up from one long side, using the paper as a guide. Place on a serving plate, with the join underneath, dust with extra icing sugar and chill for several hours before serving.

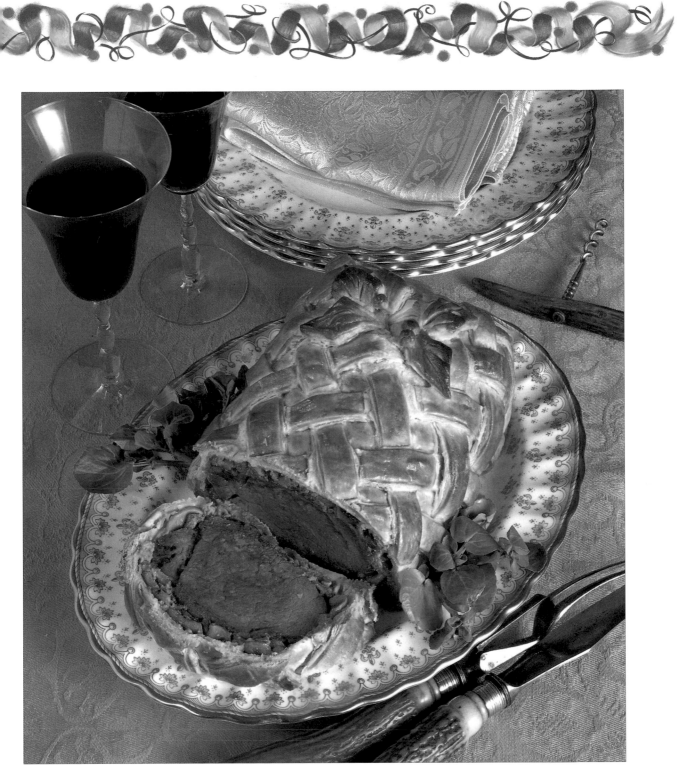

BEEF WELLINGTON

A splendid example of British cooking, this classic main course is the perfect choice for a formal dinner party or Sunday lunch gathering. It is also an excellent, and quite luxurious, alternative to Christmas turkey.

Spicy Supper Party

*F*ragrant rather than fiery, this is a menu for all palates. The quantities can easily be multiplied for an exotic buffet.

Menu for Four

SPICY FISH SLICES
PRAWN CURRY
SIMPLE TOMATO SALAD
NAN BREAD
.....
MRS BEETON'S CREAMY
CHICKEN CURRY
BASMATI RICE
SPICY SPINACH AND
CHICK PEAS
.....
LIME SORBET
ORANGE AND GRAPEFRUIT
SALAD (PAGE 25)

Most of these spicy dishes can be cooked ahead: the chicken curry may be prepared to the final stages, leaving only the cream to be added just before serving; the spice paste and sauce for the prawn curry can also be made in advance, and the shellfish stirred in and heated just before serving. The only recipe that demands last-minute attention is Spicy Fish Slices. The strips of fish can be marinated in advance but must be served freshly fried.

SIMPLE TOMATO SALAD

Serve sliced tomatoes, seasoned with salt and pepper, topped with thinly sliced or chopped onion with the fish slices. Add a sprinkling of chopped fresh coriander leaves.

BASMATI RICE

Basmati rice has a delicate fragrance and flavour which is delicious with curries and spiced dishes. Wash the rice in several changes of cold water by swirling the grains gently, then draining off the water when it becomes cloudy.

Place the rice in a saucepan, allowing 50 g/2 oz per person and adding 600 ml/1 pint for 225 g/8 oz rice. Sprinkle in a little salt and bring the water to the boil, then reduce the heat to the minimum setting and cover the pan tightly. Cook the rice for 15 minutes, then turn

the heat off and leave the pan, without removing the lid, for a further 10 minutes. Fork up the grains of rice and serve.

LIME SORBET

Follow the recipe for Lemon Sorbet (page 86), substituting the grated rind of 2 limes and fresh lime juice for the lemons. Make the sorbet at least a day before the meal so that it is properly frozen. Chill sundae glasses in the refrigerator. Use a melon scoop to shape balls of sorbet, lay them on a tray covered with cling film and replace them in the freezer. When you are ready to serve the dessert, simply pile the balls of sorbet into the chilled glasses.

Spicy Fish Slices

If cod is not available, haddock or whiting fillet may be used for this recipe. For a more pronounced fish flavour, mackerel can also be used; however, since the fillets are thinner they have to be handled with care during cooking to prevent them from breaking up.

SERVES 4

450 g/1 lb cod fillet
5 ml/1 tsp salt
3.75 ml/¾ tsp turmeric
3.75 ml/¾ tsp chilli powder
60 ml/4 tbsp oil
fresh coriander sprigs, to garnish
lemon wedges, to serve

Cut the fish into 2 cm/¾ inch slices and spread them out in a shallow dish large enough to hold all the slices in a single layer. Mix the salt and spices in a bowl. Stir in enough water to make a thick paste. Rub the paste into the fish, cover and leave to marinate for 1 hour.

Heat the oil in a large frying pan. Add as much of the spiced fish as possible, but do not overfill the pan. Fry the fish for 5–10 minutes until golden brown all over, then remove from the pan with a slotted spoon. Drain on absorbent kitchen paper and keep hot while cooking the rest of the fish.

Garnish the fish slices with fresh coriander. Serve with the tomato salad and offer lemon wedges so that their juice may be squeezed over the fish.

Prawn Curry

This curry can be made with tiger prawns, a larger, firm variety with a good flavour. Tiger prawns have striped markings and they are readily available frozen. Regardless of the choice of prawns, it is important to avoid overcooking them or they will shrivel and toughen. Do not allow the curry to boil once the prawns have been added, and simmer them long enough only to thoroughly heat and flavour them.

SERVES 4

15 ml/1 tbsp ground coriander
2.5 ml/½ tsp ground cumin
2.5 ml/½ tsp chilli powder
2.5 ml/½ tsp turmeric
1 garlic clove, crushed
250 ml/8 fl oz fish stock or water
30 ml/2 tbsp oil
1 large onion, finely chopped
45 ml/3 tbsp tomato purée
2 tomatoes, peeled, seeded and chopped
450 g/1 lb peeled cooked prawns
juice of ½ lemon
10 ml/2 tsp instant coconut milk powder (optional)
fresh coriander sprigs, to garnish

Mix all the spices in a small bowl. Add the garlic and mix to a paste with a little of the stock or water. Set aside.

Heat the oil in a frying pan, add the onion and fry for 4–5 minutes. Add the tomato purée and the spice mixture, then cook for 1–2 minutes. Stir in the remaining stock and the tomatoes, cover the pan and simmer gently for 20 minutes.

Add the prawns and lemon juice to the pan, with the coconut milk powder, if used. Stir until the powder dissolves, then simmer for 5 minutes more. Garnish with fresh coriander sprigs and serve.

INSTANT COCONUT MILK POWDER

This is a fine powder which can be substituted for coconut milk or creamed coconut. More convenient than blocks of creamed coconut, it is easily measured in small amounts and dissolves quickly.

Mrs Beeton's Creamy Chicken Curry

This curry can be made using chicken quarters, thigh joints, drumsticks or boneless breast fillets. Part-boned breasts are a good choice, providing a generous portion of meat and holding their shape well during cooking.

SERVES 4

4 part-boned chicken breasts
15 ml/1 tbsp good-quality curry powder
15 ml/1 tbsp plain flour
salt and pepper
50 g/2 oz butter
3 onions, sliced
1 eating apple, peeled, cored and diced
1 garlic clove, crushed
1 bay leaf
600 ml/1 pint chicken stock
125 ml/4 fl oz single cream
15 ml/1 tbsp lemon juice
30 ml/2 tbsp chopped fresh coriander leaves

Place the chicken in a large dish and sprinkle with the curry powder, flour and plenty of salt and pepper.

Melt half the butter in a large flameproof casserole or heavy-bottomed saucepan. Fry a third of the sliced onions in the butter until golden brown, turning the slices occasionally. Use a slotted spoon to remove the slices from the pan and set them aside.

Brown the chicken pieces in the fat remaining in the pan, reserving any flour and curry powder mixture which is left in the dish, then set them aside. Add the remaining butter to the pan. When the butter has melted, cook the remaining onions, apple, garlic and bay leaf, stirring frequently, until the mixture begins to brown. Stir in any remaining flour and curry powder, then pour in the stock and bring the sauce to the boil, stirring continuously.

Replace the chicken pieces in the pan and reduce the heat so that the sauce simmers gently. Cover the pan and cook the chicken for 45 minutes, or until tender and cooked through.

Stir in the cream and lemon juice and heat the curry gently without boiling. Taste the sauce for seasoning. Remove the bay leaf and serve the curry sprinkled with chopped coriander.

CURRY POWDER

Authentically, for an Indian curry the cook would prepare a mixture of ground spices. Typically, this would include coriander, cumin, fenugreek, chilli and turmeric. The curry would also be flavoured with whole green cardamoms and, possibly, a cinnamon stick or cassia bark.

There are many varieties of commercial curry powder: the lurid yellow, inexpensive spice is best avoided in favour of a superior brand. Add 4 green cardamoms and a cinnamon stick to the curry if you have these whole spices and remove them just before serving the dish.

Spicy Spinach and Chick Peas

SERVES 4–6

25 g/1 oz butter
30 ml/2 tbsp cumin seeds
15 ml/1 tbsp coriander seeds, crushed
15 ml/1 tbsp mustard seeds
1 large onion, chopped
2 garlic cloves, crushed
2 (425 g/15 oz) cans chick-peas, drained
5 ml/1 tsp turmeric
1 kg/2¼ lb fresh spinach, cooked
salt and pepper

Melt the butter in a saucepan. Add the cumin, coriander and mustard seeds and cook gently, stirring, for about 3 minutes or until the seeds are aromatic. Keep the heat low to avoid burning the butter.

Add the onion and garlic to the pan and continue to cook for about 15 minutes, until the onion is softened. Stir in the chick-peas and turmeric and cook for 5 minutes, until thoroughly hot. Tip the spinach into the pan and stir it over moderate heat until heated through. Season and serve.

SEAFOOD DUO

Two light seafood dishes together bring variety of flavour and texture to the first course of a delicious spicy menu.

A menu to illustrate the art of matching simple dishes with flair to make a memorable meal ... and introducing vegetarian or traditional options to suit all tastes.

Menu for Six

PAIR OF PÂTÉS
HOT TOAST
.....
CARBONNADE OF BEEF
OR
CHICK PEA CASSEROLE
BUTTERED NOODLES
ITALIAN SPINACH
.....
DEAN'S CREAM

This versatile menu is likely to become a favourite standby. The pair of pâtés is a winning first course, comprising a smoked mackerel recipe which is rich with tomato, and an egg and dill mixture to complement the fish pâté to perfection.

Vegetarians can opt to serve just the egg pâté in the confidence that it makes a delicious starter. Select one main dish, either the carbonnade or the chick-pea dish if you are making a vegetarian meal.

Lightly cooked spinach is the ideal foil for long-cooked casseroles, contributing its own particular freshness to the meal. For speed, look out for bags of baby spinach that are picked over and washed ready for cooking: simply pierce the bag and cook the spinach in the microwave following the packet instructions. Draining the spinach is simply a matter of holding the bag with a folded tea-towel and tipping out the liquid through the hole made to allow the steam to escape. The results are excellent.

Buy fresh noodles, if possible, rather than using a dried variety;. they cook in just 2–3 minutes and taste wonderful. Top the hot pasta with a large knob of butter and sprinkle with plenty of chopped fresh parsley both for colour and flavour, adding a good grinding of black pepper to pep up the dish.

Dean's cream is a real treat – an old-fashioned trifle-type recipe with a good whiff of sherry and brandy. If your guests are not renowned for their hearty appetites, offer a bowl of fresh fruit as an alternative to dessert.

SERVING THE PAIR OF PÂTÉS

Use a dessertspoon to scoop a neat oval portion of each pâté on to each plate. Garnish the pâtés with fresh herb sprigs – basil, dill and chives look very attractive overlapping thin lemon slices.

Smoked Mackerel Pâté

SERVES 4–6

25 g/1 oz butter
1 shallot, finely chopped
15 ml/1 tbsp tomato purée
1.25 ml/¼ tsp soft light brown sugar
15 ml/1 tbsp lemon juice
5 ml/1 tsp chopped fresh tarragon
4 large fresh basil leaves, finely shredded
225 g/8 oz smoked mackerel fillets, skinned
30 ml/2 tbsp double cream
few drops of Tabasco sauce
salt and pepper

Melt the butter in a saucepan, add the shallot and cook over gentle heat for 2–3 minutes. Add the tomato purée, sugar, lemon juice and tarragon and cook for 4–5 minutes. Remove from the heat, then add the basil.

Roughly purée the shallot mixture, mackerel fillets and cream in a blender or food processor. Stir in Tabasco, salt and pepper to taste, then turn the mixture into a dish and chill until firm.

Egg Pâté with Dill

SERVES 4–6

6 eggs, hard boiled
30 ml/2 tbsp chopped fresh dill
30 ml/2 tbsp snipped fresh chives
1 pickled cocktail gherkin, finely chopped
grated rind of ½ lemon
45 ml/3 tbsp plain yogurt
100 g/4 oz unsalted butter
salt and freshly ground black pepper

Mash the eggs with a fork or potato masher; alternatively, chop them very finely in a food processor, but take care not to reduce them to a paste. Mix the dill, chives, gherkins and lemon rind with the eggs. Stir in the yogurt.

Cream the butter until it is very soft, then gradually add the egg mixture, beating in each addition until the ingredients are thoroughly combined. Add salt and pepper to taste, then turn the mixture into a dish and chill until firm.

Chick-pea Casserole

SERVES 4–6

350 g/12 oz chick-peas, soaked overnight in cold water to cover
30 ml/2 tbsp olive oil
1 onion, chopped
1 garlic clove, crushed
1 bay leaf
1 green pepper, seeded and sliced
225 g/8 oz white cabbage, shredded
225 g/8 oz mushrooms, sliced
1 (397g/14oz) can chopped tomatoes
2.5 ml/½ tsp ground ginger
pinch of ground cloves
salt and pepper
30 ml/2 tbsp chopped fresh mint
60 ml/4 tbsp chopped parsley

Drain the chick-peas, put them in a saucepan and add fresh water to cover. Do not add salt. Bring to the boil,

cook for 10 minutes, then lower the heat and simmer for 1 hour or until tender. Drain the chick-peas, reserving the cooking liquor.

Heat the olive oil in a large saucepan, add the onion, garlic, bay leaf, green pepper and cabbage and fry over moderate heat for 10 minutes. Add the mushrooms, chick-peas and tomatoes. Stir in 125 ml/4 fl oz of the reserved cooking liquor, with the ginger and ground cloves. Add salt and pepper to taste. Bring to the boil, lower the heat and cook very gently for 1 hour, adding more liquid, if required, during cooking. The cooked casserole should be moist, but there should not be too much liquid. Before serving, stir in the mint, parsley and more seasoning if necessary.

Italian Spinach

SERVES 4–6

25 g/1 oz sultanas
1 kg/2¼ lb spinach
30 ml/2 tbsp oil
1 garlic clove, crushed
salt and pepper
25 g/1 oz pine nuts

Put the sultanas in a small bowl or mug, pour on boiling water to cover and set aside for 2–3 minutes until plumped. Drain well and set the sultanas aside.

Wash the fresh spinach several times and remove any coarse stalks. Put into a saucepan with just the water that clings to the leaves, then cover the pan. Put the pan over high heat for 2–3 minutes, shaking it frequently. Lower the heat, stir the spinach and cook for a further 5 minutes, turning the spinach occasionally, until cooked to your liking. Drain thoroughly, then chop the spinach coarsely.

Heat the oil in a large frying pan. Add the spinach and garlic, with salt and pepper to taste. Turn the spinach over and over in the pan with a wide spatula to heat it thoroughly without frying. Turn into a heated serving bowl, add the sultanas and nuts and mix lightly. Serve at once.

Carbonnade of Beef

Brown ale and long, slow cooking combine to make this classic, full-flavoured stew with its crunchy topping of mustard-seasoned French bread.

SERVES 6

50 g/2 oz butter or 45 ml/3 tbsp oil
675 g/1½ lb stewing steak, trimmed and cut into cubes
2 large onions, sliced
1 garlic clove, crushed
15 ml/1 tbsp plain flour
250 ml/8 fl oz beef stock
375 ml/13 fl oz brown ale
salt and pepper
1 bouquet garni
pinch of grated nutmeg
pinch of soft light brown sugar
5 ml/1 tsp red wine vinegar
6 thin slices of French bread
15 ml/1 tbsp French mustard

Set the oven at 160°C/325°F/gas 3. Melt the butter or heat the oil in a heavy-bottomed frying pan, add the beef and fry quickly until browned on all sides. Using a slotted spoon, transfer the beef to a casserole and keep hot. Add the onions to the fat remaining in the pan and fry until lightly browned, then stir in the garlic and fry over gentle heat for 1 minute.

Pour off any excess fat from the pan to leave about 15 ml/1 tbsp. Add the flour to the onions and garlic and cook, stirring constantly, until lightly browned. Gradually stir in the stock and ale, with salt and pepper to taste. Add the bouquet garni, nutmeg, brown sugar and vinegar. Bring to the boil, then pour the liquid over the beef in the casserole. Cover and bake for 2½ hours or until the beef is tender. Remove the bouquet garni.

Spread the French bread slices with mustard. Arrange them, mustard side up, on top of the carbonnade, pressing them down so that they absorb the gravy. Return the casserole to the oven, uncovered, for about 15 minutes or until the bread browns slightly. Alternatively, brown the bread topping under a hot grill for a few minutes. Serve while the bread is freshly cooked.

Dean's Cream

This is a very old recipe for a dessert that was one of the forerunners of the standard modern trifle.

SERVES 6

4 individual sponge cakes
raspberry jam
apricot jam
100 g/4 oz ratafias
150 ml/¼ pint sherry
45 ml/3 tbsp brandy
300 ml/½ pint double cream
25 g/1 oz caster sugar
DECORATION
angelica
glacé cherries
crystallized pineapple

Cut the sponge cakes in half lengthways, and spread half with raspberry jam and half with apricot jam. Arrange them in a deep glass dish, jam sides upwards.

Break the ratafias into pieces and sprinkle on top of the sponge cakes. Pour the sherry over the cakes and leave to soak for about 30 minutes.

Put the brandy, cream, and sugar into a bowl and whisk until very thick. Pile into the dish and decorate with angelica, cherries, and crystallized pineapple. Chill well before serving.

CHICK-PEA CASSEROLE AND ITALIAN SPINACH

Two colourful dishes to serve as part of a simple vegetarian meal. Alternatively, substitute a meaty casserole for the chick-pea dish to make a favourite meat-based menu.

A light menu based on fish or seafood is ideal for Christmas Eve, or any other occasion that precedes a period of feasting, either as a family meal or for an informal supper party.

Menu for Four

TOMATO AND SPRING ONION DIP
HERB DIP
CRUDITÉS
.....
MONKFISH AND BACON KEBABS
LEMON PARSLEY RICE
PEPPER SALAD
WARM CRUSTY BREAD
.....
LEMON SORBET WITH MELON

CRUDITÉS

Cut fingers of carrot, celery and cucumber to serve with the dip. Cherry tomatoes, radishes, grapes and halved and stoned fresh dates are also tempting with the creamy herb mixture. Mini breadsticks and rice cakes may be added to the selection of crudités.

LEMON SORBET WITH MELON

Buy 2 small melons, such as Ogen or Galia, and cut them in half using the Vandyke cutting technique to give an attractive zig-zag top (page 13). Scoop out the seeds carefully to avoid spoiling the cut edges and chill the fruit.

Use a melon scoop to make small balls of sorbet, placing them on a tray lined with clingfilm, then return them to the freezer until you are ready to serve the dessert. Pile the balls of sorbet on the melon halves and serve immediately.

Tomato and Spring Onion Dip

SERVES 4

4 ripe tomatoes, peeled
5 ml/1 tsp tomato purée
2.5 ml/½ teaspoon caster sugar
salt and pepper
freshly grated nutmeg
15 ml/1 tbsp walnut or hazelnut oil
225 g/8 oz ricotta cheese
2 spring onions, finely chopped

Halve the tomatoes and scoop out their seeds, then finely chop the flesh and set it aside. In a bowl, mix the tomato purée with the sugar, salt and freshly ground black pepper, and a little nutmeg. Stir in the nut oil. When the tomato purée is thoroughly combined with the other ingredients, add the ricotta cheese and mix well.

Stir the chopped tomatoes and spring onions into the mixture, then taste it and add more seasoning or nutmeg if necessary. Chill the dip for at least an hour before serving.

Herb Dip

45 ml/3 tbsp snipped chives
30 ml/2 tbsp finely chopped parsley
grated rind of ½ lemon
100 g/4 oz cream cheese
150 ml/¼ pint mayonnaise
150 ml/¼ pint fromage frais or soured cream
salt and pepper

Mix the chives, parsley and lemon rind with the cream cheese. Stir in the mayonnaise and fromage frais or soured cream. Add a little salt and pepper to taste.

Transfer the dip to a serving dish, cover and chill for at least 2 hours before serving. The dip tastes best when chilled overnight.

VARIETIES OF SOFT CHEESE FOR DIPS

There is a wide choice of soft cheese, all perfectly suitable for making dips, but each giving a slightly different result.

Cream Cheese Sold loose or in tubs, sometimes labelled 'full-fat soft cheese', this is the richest choice with a high fat content. Cream cheese has a heavy , sometimes buttery, texture and it has to be thinned slightly so that ingredients can be dipped in it.

Medium-fat Soft Cheese Not as heavy as cream cheese, but quite thick and fairly rich, usually giving a dip a rich taste. Quark is a medium-fat soft cheese with a slightly dry flavour.

Low-fat Soft Cheese This may be sold loose at delicatessen counters or it is available in branded tubs. The loose cheese can be quite soft in texture and weak in flavour. Branded low-fat cheeses sometimes have a 'processed' flavour and some have a starchy texture. Curd cheese is a good choice of low-fat soft cheese as it has a medium-thick texture and it tastes quite creamy, but there is a tangy edge to its flavour.

Fromage Frais Fresh cheese, this has a dropping consistency more like thick cream than soft cheese. The fat content varies: high-fat fromage frais is rich and quite luscious, medium-fat varieties are quite creamy and the low-fat or virtually-fat-free fromage frais is very light in flavour and texture.

Monkfish and Bacon Kebabs

Wooden or bamboo skewers may be used for these kebabs, but they must be soaked in water to prevent them from scorching under the grill. Metal skewers are less trouble, and the food can also be threaded on them several hours in advance and chilled.

75 ml/3 fl oz olive oil
1 garlic clove, crushed
5 ml/1 tsp lemon juice
5 ml/1 tsp dried oregano
575 g/1¼ lb monkfish, cleaned, trimmed and cut into
2 cm/¾ inch cubes
225 g/8 oz rindless streaky bacon rashers
225 g/8 oz button mushrooms
salt and pepper
GARNISH
lime wedges
watercress sprigs

Combine the olive oil, garlic, lemon juice and oregano in a shallow bowl large enough to hold all the monkfish cubes. Mix well, add the fish, and marinate for 15 minutes.

Drain the monkfish, reserving the marinade. Thread a piece of bacon on to a metal kebab skewer. Add a cube of fish, then a mushroom, weaving the bacon between them. Continue to add the fish and mushrooms, each time interweaving the bacon, until the skewer is full. Add a second rasher of bacon if necessary. Fill three more skewers in the same way. Sprinkle with salt and pepper.

Grill the monkfish kebabs under moderate heat for 10–15 minutes, basting frequently with the reserved marinade. Serve the kebabs on a bed of rice, garnishing them with lime wedges and watercress sprigs.

Lemon Parsley Rice

SERVES 4

225 g/8 oz long-grain rice
grated rind of 1 lemon
salt
60 ml/4 tbsp chopped parsley
30 ml/2 tbsp snipped chives

Place the rice in a saucepan with the lemon rind. Add a little salt and pour in 600 ml/1 pint water. Bring to the boil and stir the rice once, then reduce the heat to the lowest setting and cover the pan tightly. Cook the rice for 20 minutes, then turn the heat off and leave it to stand, without removing the lid from the pan, for a further 5 minutes.

Sprinkle the parsley and chives over the rice and fork them into the grains, then turn out the rice into a warmed serving dish or divide it between four plates.

Pepper Salad

SERVES 4–6

1 large green pepper
1 large red pepper
1 large yellow pepper
1 small mild red or white onion, thinly sliced in rings
50 ml/2 fl oz olive oil
salt and pepper (optional)

Wash the peppers and pat dry with absorbent kitchen paper. Grill under moderate heat, turning the peppers frequently with tongs until the skins blister, then char all over. Immediately transfer the peppers to a large bowl and cover with several layers of absorbent kitchen paper. Alternatively, put the grilled peppers in a polythene bag. When cold, rub off the skin under cold water. Remove cores and seeds and cut the peppers into thin strips.

Put the pepper strips on a serving platter, arrange the onion rings around the rim, and drizzle the olive oil over the top. Add salt and pepper to taste, if liked. Serve at once.

Lemon Sorbet

SERVES 4–6

10 ml/2 tsp gelatine
150 g/5 oz caster sugar
grated rind of 1 lemon
250 ml/8 fl oz lemon juice
2 egg whites

Turn the freezing compartment or freezer to the coldest setting about 1 hour before making the sorbet.

Place 30 ml/2 tbsp water in a small bowl and sprinkle the gelatine on to the liquid. Set the bowl aside for 15 minutes until the gelatine is spongy. Stand the bowl over a pan of hot water; stir until the gelatine has dissolved.

Put the sugar in a heavy-bottomed saucepan with 200 ml/7 fl oz water. Dissolve the sugar over gentle heat, without stirring. Bring the mixture to the boil and boil gently for about 10 minutes. Stir the dissolved gelatine into the syrup, with the lemon rind and juice. Cover and cool.

Pour the cool syrup mixture into a suitable container for freezing. Cover the container closely and freeze until half-frozen.

In a clean, grease-free bowl, whisk the egg whites until stiff. Beat the sorbet mixture until smooth, scraping off any ice crystals. Fold in the egg whites, replace the cover on the bowl and freeze. The mixture should be firm enough to scoop; it will not freeze hard. Return the freezer to the normal setting.

Serve in scoops, straight from the freezer, in Vandyked melon halves, as described in the menu introduction.

MONKFISH AND BACON KEBABS

Quick-to-cook fish kebabs are the ideal alternative to heavy wintry menus for pre-Christmas supper parties.

Hearty High Tea

Alongside traditional cooked breakfasts and the Sunday roast, high tea rightly takes its place as part of British culinary heritage. Originally a family meal, this combination of tea and supper goes down well with younger and older generations alike.

Menu for Four

MRS BEETON'S SCOTCH EGGS
COLD MEAT AND CHEESE
PLATTER
SELECTION OF PICKLES AND
RELISHES
TOMATOES
BREAD AND BUTTER
.....
TOASTED CRUMPETS (PAGE 98)
OR MUFFINS
BARA BRITH
CHERRY BREAD
.....
BLANCMANGE MOULD

High tea is meant to be a practical meal, providing something savoury and satisfying followed by cakes or sweet breads and a homely dessert or pudding. Hot snacks may be served – anything from a plate of fried eggs and bacon, poached eggs or grilled mushrooms on toast to jugged kippers or a full-scale mixed grill. Fried potatoes, crisp and golden with a floury centre, are another favourite for high tea, especially to complement roasted meats and salad.

Cold meats, cheese and pickles, often served with salad, are a good choice and a large plate of thickly sliced bread spread with butter is essential. Cold cooked ham, tongue and turkey or chicken should be neatly arranged on a large platter. Salami or other continental cooked sausages may be added to the platter. British hard cheeses or sliced Emmental, Gouda and Gruyère go well with cold meats and salad.

Offer a good selection of pickles with the meat platter: Pickled Onions (page 30), pickled cabbage and pickled eggs are all popular. Add a pot of chutney and some hot English mustard to go with cold ham.

MAKING GOOD TEA

A piping-hot pot of tea is, of course, the other essential feature of high tea, made with loose tea and not modern teabags. Traditionally, each person would drink several cups of tea with the meal, so protecting the pot with a large cosy was vital, and keeping a kettle of freshly boiled water ready for topping up the pot was equally important.

• Use fresh water. Warm the pot by pouring some boiling water into it, swirling it around, and then pouring it away.

• The tradition is to allow 5 ml/1 tsp loose tea per person plus 5 ml/1 tsp per pot; however, if the tea is strong and the pot small (literally allowing 1 generous cup per person), this may be too much. Experiment to find the quantity that produces the perfect brew for your taste.

• Pour freshly boiling water from the kettle on the tea and cover the tea pot. Use a tea-cosy to keep the beverage piping hot.

• Leave the tea to brew: small-leafed varieties should be left for 3 minutes; large leaf tea for 6 minutes. When ready, the tea leaves should have sunk to the bottom of the pot.

• Use a tea strainer when pouring tea and remember a saucer or stand on which to place the strainer to avoid leftover tea dripping on the table.

• Although some teas are best enjoyed black, always offer cold milk or lemon: the latter with delicate, weak teas and scented types.

Mrs Beeton's Scotch Eggs

MAKES 4

4 rindless back bacon rashers, finely chopped
50 g/2 oz shredded suet
75 g/3 oz wholemeal breadcrumbs
15 ml/1 tbsp grated lemon rind
5 ml/1 tsp finely chopped parsley
1.25 ml/¼ tsp dried oregano
pinch of ground mace
salt and cayenne pepper
Worcestershire sauce
2 eggs, beaten
75 g/3 oz fresh white breadcrumbs
15 ml/1 tbsp plain flour, plus extra for dusting
salt and pepper
4 hard-boiled eggs
oil for deep frying

Combine the bacon, suet, breadcrumbs, lemon rind, herbs and mace in a bowl. Add salt, cayenne and Worcestershire sauce to taste. Stir in enough of the beaten egg to make a forcemeat which can be shaped.

Beat the remaining beaten egg with 10 ml/2 tsp water in a small bowl. Spread out the breadcrumbs in a second, shallow bowl. Divide the forcemeat into 4 equal pieces. On a surface lightly dusted with flour, pat each piece into a 13 cm/5 inch circle.

Mix the flour with the salt and pepper in a sturdy polythene bag. Add the hard-boiled eggs and toss gently to coat evenly. Place an egg in the centre of each circle of forcemeat. Mould the forcemeat evenly round the egg, making sure it fits snugly. Seal the joins with a little of the beaten egg mixture and pinch well together.

Mould each Scotch egg to a good shape, brush all over with beaten egg, then roll in the breadcrumbs until evenly coated. Press the crumbs well in.

Put the oil for frying into a deep saucepan and heat to 160°C/325°F or until a cube of bread added to the oil browns in 2 minutes. Add the eggs carefully and fry for about 10 minutes until golden brown. Lift out with a slotted spoon and drain on absorbent kitchen paper. Serve hot or cold.

Bara Brith

MAKES ABOUT 12 SLICES

fat for greasing
450 g/1 lb strong plain flour
75 g/3 oz lard or butter
50 g/2 oz chopped mixed peel
150 g/5 oz seedless raisins
50 g/2 oz currants
75 g/3 oz soft light brown sugar
5 ml/1 tsp ground mixed spice
1 sachet fast-action easy-blend dried yeast
pinch of salt
250 ml/8 fl oz hand-hot milk
1 egg, beaten
flour for kneading
clear honey for glazing (optional)

Grease a 20 x 13 x 7.5 cm/8 x 5 x 3 inch loaf tin. Sift the flour into a bowl and rub in the lard or butter. Stir in the peel, raisins, currants, brown sugar, mixed spice, yeast and salt.

Make a well in the centre of the dry ingredients, then add the milk and the beaten egg. Mix to a soft dough. Turn out the dough on to a floured board and knead well until smooth and elastic. Place the dough in the prepared loaf tin, pressing it well into the corners. Place the tin in a large, lightly oiled polythene bag. Leave the loaf in a warm place until doubled in volume and risen just above the rim of the tin. Set the oven at 200°C/400°F/gas 6.

Bake the bread for 15 minutes, then lower the oven temperature to 160°C/325°F/gas 3. Continue baking for about 1¼ hours. Turn out on to a wire rack and brush the top with clear honey if liked.

Cherry Bread

fat for greasing
200 g/7 oz strong white flour
2.5 ml/½ tsp salt
100 ml/3½ fl oz hand-hot milk
25 g/1 oz butter or margarine
1 egg
flour for kneading
75 g/3 oz glacé cherries
milk for glazing

Grease a 15 cm/6 inch cake tin. Sift the flour and salt into a bowl. Rub in the butter or margarine. Stir in the yeast. Make a well in the dry ingredients, then pour in the milk and add the beaten egg. Gradually mix in the dry ingredients to make a soft dough. Turn on to a lightly floured surface and knead for about 5 minutes or until the dough is smooth and no longer sticky.

Chop the cherries roughly and knead them into the dough until well distributed. Press the dough into the prepared cake tin and brush the surface with a little milk. Place the tin in a large, lightly oiled polythene bag. Leave in a warm place until the dough reaches just above the edge of the tin. Set the oven at 220°C/425°F/gas 7.

Bake for 10 minutes, then lower the oven temperature to 190°C/375°F/gas 5. Continue baking for 15–25 minutes, until golden brown. Turn out on to a wire rack to cool.

Blancmange Mould

Blancmange may be made using ground rice or arrowroot instead of the cornflour given below. The quantities will be the same. Although puddings of this type are often flavoured with chocolate or strawberry, the original blancmange was a white mould flavoured with sweet and bitter almonds.

75 g/3 oz cornflour
1 litre/1¾ pints milk
50 g/2 oz sugar
a little natural almond essence

In a bowl, blend the cornflour to a smooth paste with a little of the cold milk. Bring the remaining milk to the boil in a saucepan.

Pour the boiling milk on to the cornflour mixture, stirring all the time. Pour the mixture back into the pan and heat gently, stirring all the time until the mixture simmers and thickens. Allow to simmer for 5–10 minutes, stirring occasionally.

Remove the pan from the heat and stir in the sugar. Add almond essence to taste, stir well, then pour the blancmange into a wetted 1.1 litre/2 pint mould. Press dampened greaseproof paper or microwave cooking film on to the surface of the blancmange and cool.

Chill the cooled blancmange for at least 2 hours, or until set. Unmould the blancmange just before serving.

ARROWROOT
If arrowroot is used instead of cornflour, the pan should be removed from the heat as soon as the mixture has reached a full boil. If arrowroot is cooked for any length of time after boiling, it tends to thin down.

TRADITIONAL TEABREADS

Buttered plain or thickly sliced and toasted, teabreads are an essential feature of a traditional high tea menu.

Fuss-free Meal for Friends

*T*his is an informal
meal which can be
prepared ahead and
served without pomp and
ceremony. A meaty stew
and moist risotto – perfect
for a mid-week evening
with friends or Friday
night supper party.

Menu for Four

OSSO BUCO
RISOTTO MILANESE
GREEN SALAD (PAGE 32)
.....
MERINGUES
COFFEE ICE CREAM
HOT MOCHA SAUCE
.....
CHEESEBOARD
FRUIT BASKET

The beauty of this meal is that most of it can be cooked in advance. The Osso Buco can be frozen and the ice cream made up to 2–3 weeks before the meal. The meringues will keep perfectly well in an airtight tin in a cool room for 2–3 weeks. The Hot Mocha Sauce can also be made in advance – when cold it can be stored in an airtight container in the refrigerator for weeks. Reheat the sauce in a small saucepan or in a suitable serving jug in the microwave. If the Osso Buco is frozen, remember to thaw it overnight in a cool room or for about 24 hours in the refrigerator.

On the day of the supper party, all you will need to do is set out the cheeseboard and fruit basket, toss the salad and make the risotto.

CHEESEBOARD IDEAS

Instead of buying a selection of different cheeses, make some potted cheese or offer a soft goats' cheese with fresh figs or dates.

To pot cheese, simply grate the cheese, then pound it to a paste with a small amount of butter or soft cheese. Moisten the cheese with red wine, port, sherry, milk or cream and flavour it with chopped herbs or grated nutmeg. Pack the cheese in a small pot. This is a particularly good way of using up small pieces of cheese left over from a dinner party or the remains of a whole cheese, such as Stilton.

CUTLERY FOR EATING FRUIT

The familiar fruit (such as apples, pears and bananas) are usually eaten with a dessert fork and small knife, but some of the exotics are more easily tackled with a spoon. Papaya, guava, persimmon (or Sharon fruit) and mangosteen are cut with a knife, kiwi fruit can be cut or scooped out with a teaspoon, and a small teaspoon is essential for eating passion fruit. If possible, provide serrated knives – steak knives – for halving crisp passion fruit shells. Small, sharp knives are ideal for slitting crisp-skinned lychees.

Osso Buco

SERVES 4

450 g/1 lb tomatoes, peeled, seeded and chopped or
1 (397 g/14 oz) can chopped tomatoes
30 ml/2 tbsp tomato purée
300 ml/½ pint beef stock
salt and pepper
50 g/2 oz plain flour
4 veal knuckles or 4 veal shank slices, about
2 cm/¾ inch thick
60 ml/4 tbsp oil
1 onion, finely chopped
2 garlic cloves, crushed
2 carrots, finely chopped
2 celery sticks, sliced
juice of 1 lemon
150 ml/¼ pint dry white wine
2 bay leaves
2 fresh thyme sprigs
GREMOLADA
45 ml/3 tbsp chopped parsley
1 garlic clove, chopped
grated rind of ½ lemon

Set the oven at 180°C/350°F/gas 4. Put the tomatoes, with any juices, into a bowl. Stir in the tomato purée and stock, with salt and pepper to taste. Set the mixture aside.

Put the flour in a stout polythene bag. Season with salt and pepper. Add the veal knuckles or shank slices and toss until evenly coated. Remove the pieces of meat, shaking off the excess flour; reserve the leftover flour.

Heat the oil in a large flameproof casserole, add the meat and fry for about 8 minutes, turning once or twice, until browned all over. With tongs, transfer the meat to a plate and set aside.

Add the onion, garlic, carrots and celery to the fat remaining in the casserole. Fry for 6–8 minutes or until the onion is golden brown. Stir in the reserved flour, then gradually pour in the tomato mixture and bring to the boil, stirring continuously and scraping in any sediment on the base of the pan. Stir in the lemon juice and wine, with the bay leaves and thyme.

Return the veal to the casserole, pushing the pieces well down so that they are completely covered by the sauce. Cover the dish tightly with foil and a lid and bake for 1½–2 hours or until the meat is very tender. Remove the bay leaves and thyme sprigs. If necessary, place the casserole over moderate heat for 5–10 minutes, stirring occasionally, to reduce the sauce.

Make the gremolada by mixing all the ingredients together in a small bowl. Sprinkle over the osso buco just before serving.

Risotto Milanese

SERVES 4

75 g/3 oz butter
30 ml/2 tbsp olive oil
1 onion, finely chopped
350 g/12 oz risotto rice
600 ml/1 pint vegetable stock
2.5 ml/½ tsp saffron threads
300 ml/½ pint dry white wine
salt and pepper
150 g/5 oz Parmesan cheese, grated

Heat 25 g/1 oz of the butter with the olive oil in a large saucepan. Add the onion and fry gently, stirring occasionally, for 10 minutes. Add the rice and cook for a few minutes, stirring gently until all the rice grains are coated in fat. Meanwhile heat the stock to simmering point in a separate pan.

Put the saffron threads in a mortar and pound them with a pestle. Stir in a little of the hot stock to dissolve the saffron, then set aside.

Add the wine and half the remaining stock to the rice, with salt and pepper to taste. Bring to the boil. Stir once, lower the heat and cover the pan tightly. Leave over low heat for 10 minutes. Pour in half the remaining hot stock, do not stir, then cover and cook for 5 minutes, shaking the pan occasionally to prevent sticking. Finally, add the remaining stock and saffron liquid. Stir once or twice, cover and cook for about 10 minutes, until the rice is cooked, creamy and moist.

Stir in the remaining butter and the cheese. Taste the risotto, adding more salt and pepper if required. Cover tightly and leave to stand for 5 minutes before serving.

Meringues

This basic meringue mixture may also be used for cases and toppings.

MAKES 24–30

4 egg whites
pinch of salt
200 g/7 oz caster sugar, plus extra for dusting
1.25 ml/¼ tsp baking powder (optional)
whipped cream, to fill (optional)

Line a baking sheet with oiled greaseproof paper or with non-stick baking parchment. Set the oven at 110°C/225°F/gas ¼.

Combine the egg whites and salt in a large grease-free bowl and whisk until the whites are very stiff and standing in points. They must be completely dry. Gradually add half the caster sugar, 15 ml/1 tbsp at a time, whisking well after each addition until the meringue is stiff. If the sugar is not thoroughly blended in it will form droplets of syrup which may brown, spoiling the appearance and texture of the meringues, and making them difficult to remove from the paper when cooked.

When half the sugar has been whisked in, sprinkle the rest over the surface of the mixture and, using a metal spoon, fold it in very lightly with the baking powder, if used. Put the meringue mixture into a piping bag fitted with a large nozzle and pipe into rounds on the paper. Alternatively, shape the mixture using two wet tablespoons. Take up a spoonful of the mixture and smooth it with a palette knife, bringing it up into a ridge in the centre. Slide it out with the other spoon on to the prepared baking sheet, with the ridge on top.

Dust the meringues lightly with caster sugar, then dry off in the oven for 3–4 hours, until they are firm and crisp but still white. If the meringues begin to brown, prop the oven door open a little. When they are crisp on the outside, lift the meringues carefully off the sheet, using a palette knife. Turn them on to their sides and return to the oven until the bases are dry. Cool on a wire rack. If you like, the meringues can be sandwiched together with whipped cream. Filled meringues should be served within 1 hour or they will soften.

Coffee Ice Cream

SERVES 4

45 ml/3 tbsp instant coffee powder
300 ml/½ pint double cream
75 g/3 oz caster sugar

Turn the freezing compartment or freezer to the coldest setting about 1 hour before making the ice cream.

Pour 60 ml/4 tbsp boiling water into a cup, add the instant coffee and stir until dissolved. Set aside until cool.

Whip the cream in a bowl until stiff. Stir in the sugar and fold in the dissolved coffee. Spoon into a suitable container for freezing. Cover the container closely and freeze until half frozen (when ice crystals appear around the edge of the mixture). Beat the ice cream until smooth, scraping off any crystals. Replace the cover and freeze until firm. Return the freezer to the normal setting.

Transfer the ice cream to the refrigerator about 15 minutes before serving, to allow it to soften and 'ripen'. Serve in individual dishes or in a large bowl.

Hot Mocha Sauce

SERVES 4

150 ml/¼ pint very strong black coffee
75 g/3 oz sugar
225 g/8 oz dark plain chocolate

Heat the coffee and sugar in a small saucepan, stirring until the sugar melts. Bring to a full boil and cook for 1 minute, then remove the pan from the heat.

Break the chocolate into squares and add them to the coffee syrup. Stir until the chocolate melts, replacing the pan over low heat if necessary. Serve hot.

OSSO BUCO WITH RISOTTO MILANESE

Planning the menu around a prepare-ahead casserole leaves the cook free to enjoy an informal evening's entertaining to the full.

Afternoon Tea Party

An old-fashioned afternoon tea party provides the perfect opportunity for indulging in favourite treats, and will be enjoyed by adults and children alike.

Menu for Eight

SANDWICH SELECTION
·····
TOASTED CRUMPETS
·····
PASTRY HORNS
VOLS-AU-VENT
·····
DUNDEE CAKE
·····
TEA WITH MILK OR LEMON
TEA PUNCH

Afternoon tea can include a wide variety of breads, cakes, pastries and biscuits, but it can be a mistake to prepare too much sweet food without balancing the menu with sandwiches or other savouries. Home-made crumpets are a terrific treat for winter teas – especially if you can sit in front of an open fire to toast them.

If preferred, the crumpets can be cooked and cooled, then frozen in a sealed polythene bag. They will keep very well for at least 6 months. The crumpets can be toasted from frozen under the grill or at a distance from a red-hot fire: but do not hold them too close to the heat or they will brown before thawing.

The pastry horns can also be prepared ahead and frozen, but they are fragile, so must be packed in rigid containers. When serving, crisp the pastry by heating the horns briefly in a hot oven.

SANDWICH SELECTION

Prepare two or three types of sandwiches, with fairly plain fillings for afternoon tea. Cucumber, smoked salmon, ham and mustard or egg and cress are all suitable fillings. Use fresh bread and soften the butter so that it is easy to spread thinly. Cut the crusts off the bread first, then they can be reduced to breadcrumbs and frozen for future use.

Cucumber Peel and thinly slice the cucumber, place the slices in a shallow dish or on a plate, sprinkle them with a little vinegar and leave them to stand for 10–15 minutes. Flavour the butter with some finely snipped chives, if liked. Drain the cucumber, mop it with absorbent kitchen paper and season the sandwiches, with salt and freshly ground black pepper.

Smoked Salmon Flavour the butter with chopped dill and parsley, or parsley and chives, if liked. The sandwiches are best left open, with the slices of smoked salmon neatly pressed on medium-thick slices of bread, and cut in half. Serve with lemon wedges.

Ham and Mustard Cream the butter with prepared English mustard or spread the mustard on the buttered bread. Trim excess fat from the ham

Egg and Cress Snip the tops off mustard and cress and mix with mashed hard-boiled eggs, adding mayonnaise to bind the ingredients. Add salt and pepper to taste.

REFRESHING TEA IDEAS

Brew a delicate variety of tea, such as Earl Grey or Darjeeling, and serve with a choice of milk or thin slices of lemon. Alternatively, try one of the fruit-flavoured teas. Spiced and Christmas varieties of tea are especially festive, and they taste wonderful with fruit cake (or mince pies). Thinly sliced orange may be served with spiced teas.

To make a simple tea punch, add orange and lemon slices and a small amount of sugar to freshly brewed fruit-flavoured tea or spiced tea. Cool the mixture swiftly by adding ice cubes, then leave it until cold. Top up with an equal quantity of sparkling or semi-sparkling white wine, add more ice and serve. Dry or medium dry cider is also good with tea in a punch. Taste the punch for sweetness before serving.

Pastry Horns

MAKES 8

**225 g/8 oz puff pastry, thawed if frozen
flour for rolling out
beaten egg and milk for glazing**

Roll out the pastry on a lightly floured surface to a thickness of 5 mm/¼ inch, then cut into strips 35 cm/ 14 inches long and 2 cm/¾ inch wide. Moisten the strips with cold water.

Wind each strip around a cornet mould, working from the point upward, keeping the moistened surface on the outside. Lay the horns on a dampened baking sheet, with the final overlap of the pastry strip underneath. Leave in a cool place for 1 hour.

Set the oven at 220°C/425°F/gas 7. Brush the horns with beaten egg and milk. Bake for 10–15 minutes or until golden brown. Remove the moulds and return the horns to the oven for 5 minutes. Cool completely on a wire rack. When cold, fill the horns with a sweet or savoury filling.

Vol-au-vent Cases

MAKES 12

**225 g/8 oz puff pastry, thawed if frozen
flour for rolling out
beaten egg for glazing**

Set the oven at 220°C/425°F/gas 7. Roll out the pastry on a lightly floured surface to a thickness of about 1 cm/½ inch. Use a 5 cm/2 inch round cutter to stamp out circles of pastry. Place on a baking sheet and brush the top of the pastry with beaten egg.

With a smaller, floured cutter, make a circular cut in each case, to form an inner ring, cutting through about half the depth of the pastry. Bake for 20–25 minutes until golden brown and crisp.

When baked, remove the inner circular lid, then scoop out the soft inside while still warm to make room for a sweet or savoury filling.

SAVOURY AND SWEET FILLINGS

Seafood Filling For vol-au-vent cases. Melt 25 g/1 oz butter in a saucepan. Stir in 25 g/1 oz plain flour, then cook for 1 minute. Pour in 300 ml/½ pint milk, stirring all the time, and bring to the boil. Simmer for 3 minutes. Drain a 200 g/7 oz can of tuna and add it to the sauce with 100 g/4 oz frozen peeled cooked prawns. Add salt and pepper to taste. Stir in 30 ml/ 2 tbsp chopped parsley and simmer for 3 minutes, stirring occasionally, until the prawns are thawed. Spoon into the pastry cases and serve hot.

Hot Chicken Make the sauce as for the seafood filling, using half milk and half chicken stock. Instead of adding tuna, stir in 225 g/8 oz diced cooked chicken meat and 50 g/2 oz sliced button mushrooms. Season with a little nutmeg, then simmer gently for 5 minutes. Stir in 60 ml/4 tbsp single cream and a little chopped tarragon or parsley. Heat gently but do not boil. Spoon into the pastry cases and serve hot.

Ham and Tomato Mix 50 g/2 oz diced cooked ham with 2 diced, peeled tomatoes, 1 chopped spring onion and 100 g/4 oz soft cheese (full-fat soft cheese, ricotta, quark or low-fat soft cheese). Add salt and pepper to taste, then spoon into the cold pastry cases.

Chicken Mayonnaise Bind 100 g/4 oz diced cooked chicken with mayonnaise to a creamy mixture. Add 30 ml/2 tbsp snipped chives and salt and pepper to taste, then spoon into the cold pastry cases.

Spiced Turkey Dice 100–175 g/4–6 oz cooked turkey and mix with 15 ml/1 tbsp mango chutney. Cook ½ chopped onion in 25 g/1 oz butter until soft, stir in 5 ml/1 tsp curry powder and cook for 2 minutes. Stir into the turkey, then bind with mayonnaise.

Jam and Cream Place 5 ml/1 tsp jam in each pastry case, then top with whipped cream. The cream may be flavoured with a little liqueur (such as Grand Marnier) or sherry and sweetened with a little caster or icing sugar before whipping.

Fruit Horns Roughly chopped fresh fruit, such as strawberries or peaches, may be mixed with lightly sweetened whipped cream to fill the pastry cases.

Chocolate Cream Stir 45 ml/3 tbsp boiling water into 15 ml/1 tbsp cocoa. Add 30 ml/2 tbsp brandy or chocolate liqueur. Mix in 300 ml/½ pint double cream and 30 ml/2 tbsp icing sugar. Whip the cream until it stands in soft peaks. Pipe or spoon it into the pastries.

Crumpets

MAKES 10–12

200 g/7 oz strong white flour
2.5 ml/½ tsp salt
1 sachet fast-action easy-blend dried yeast
100 ml/3½ fl oz milk
pinch of bicarbonate of soda
fat for frying

Sift the flour and salt into a large bowl. Stir in the yeast and make a well in the centre. Heat the milk with 125 ml/4 fl oz water until hand hot. Pour the mixture into the well in the dry ingredients. Gradually mix in the dry ingredients, then beat hard to make a smooth, elastic batter. Cover the bowl with cling film and leave in a warm place for about 45 minutes or until the batter has doubled in bulk.

Dissolve the bicarbonate of soda in 45 ml/3 tbsp warm water; beat into the batter. Heat a griddle or heavy-bottomed frying pan over medium heat, then grease it when hot. Grease metal crumpet rings, poaching rings or large plain biscuit cutters about 7.5 cm/3 inches in diameter. Place the rings on the hot griddle, pour a spoonful of batter into each to cover the base thinly and cook until the top is set and the bubbles have burst.

Remove the rings and turn the crumpets over. Cook the other side for 2–3 minutes only, until firm but barely coloured. Cool the crumpets on a wire rack. Serve toasted, with butter.

Dundee Cake

MAKES ONE 18 CM/7 INCH CAKE

fat for greasing
200 g/7 oz plain flour
2.5 ml/½ tsp baking powder
1.25 ml/¼ tsp salt
150 g/5 oz butter
150 g/5 oz caster sugar
4 eggs, beaten
100 g/4 oz glacé cherries, quartered
150 g/5 oz currants
150 g/5 oz sultanas
100 g/4 oz seedless raisins
50 g/2 oz cut mixed peel
50 g/2 oz ground almonds
grated rind of 1 lemon
50 g/2 oz blanched split almonds

Line and grease an 18 cm/7 inch round cake tin. Set the oven at 180°C/350°F/gas 4. Sift the flour, baking powder and salt into a bowl. In a mixing bowl, cream the butter and sugar together well, and beat in the eggs. Fold the flour mixture, cherries, dried fruit, peel and ground almonds into the creamed mixture. Add the lemon rind and mix well.

Spoon into the prepared tin and make a slight hollow in the centre. Bake for 20 minutes, by which time the hollow should have filled in. Arrange the split almonds on top.

Bake the cake for a further 40–50 minutes, then reduce the temperature to 160°C/325°F/gas 3 and bake for 1 hour more. Cool on a wire rack.

PASTRY HORNS AND VOLS-AU-VENT

*With bought puff pastry, baking an array of tempting light pastries is not necessarily a time-consuming task –
and they are the perfect choice for afternoon tea.*

> *S*wing into the party season with this tasty collection of cocktail snacks which look and taste impressive without frantic last-minute preparation.

Menu for Twelve

VEGETABLE CRUDITÉS
·····
ANGELS ON HORSEBACK
(PAGE 33)
·····
CURRY CHEESE TOPPERS
BURLINGTON CROÛTES
ANCHOVY APPETIZERS
·····
CHEESE BUTTERFLIES
CHEESE STRAWS
·····
WHITE OR RED WINE
SELECTION OF ALCOHOL-FREE
DRINKS

Inviting trays of tempting savouries look deceptively simple to prepare – in practice they can be time-consuming and fiddly. Careful planning is essential if you want to avoid spending hours in the kitchen just before a cocktail party. Balance the workload by including a range of savouries that can be prepared the day before (or earlier) alongside some which require last-minute attention. Take a realistic view of your ability and speed when handling tiny garnishes, and persuade someone to help if you are likely to panic at the last minute.

It is a good idea to include a platter or two of vegetable crudités as they cleanse the palate and make a change from pastries, cheese snacks and rich savouries. Celery, cucumber and carrot sticks and wedges of fennel are all ideal, as are whole radishes and cherry tomatoes. There is no need to offer a dip (which would completely change the character of the savoury), but a sprinkling of grated nutmeg, paprika, chilli powder or garam masala (ground roasted spices) would add an interesting hint of seasoning.

SERVING COCKTAIL SNACKS

Large trays are easy to hand around and are ideal when offering the first wave of snacks, but as the party progresses it is best to serve off plates to avoid partially emptied trays being left to one side. Polite guests often prefer not to finish the last couple of items on a dish, so make a point of clearing away platters that are almost empty, transferring the savouries to full plates.

Encourage a few good friends to help themselves to snacks and to pass plates around if you do not want to spend the entire evening waiting on guests. If you are planning a large or formal gathering, it is worth hiring a professional waiter or bartender to help with drinks and to serve refreshments.

DRINKS

When mixing cocktails, select two or three different recipes and stock up your bar accordingly. It is a mistake to buy a vast array of different drinks and launch into your own – unplanned – happy hour. Always offer thirst-quenching long drinks and alcohol-free alternatives as this is important for everyone, not just essential for drivers.

Chilled champagne or sparkling wine may be served instead of cocktails. Sherry, vermouth and spirits with mixers are also acceptable; however, the general trend is towards drinking wine instead of stronger beverages.

Cold beer (including an alcohol-free variety) should always be available, along with fruit juices and sparkling mineral water.

Curry Cheese Toppers

MAKES 12

30 ml/2 tbsp apricot or mango chutney
175 g/6 oz mature Cheddar cheese, grated
5 ml/1 tsp curry paste
12 large water biscuits or Bath Oliver biscuits

Chop any large chunks in the chutney. Pound the cheese, chutney and curry paste together in a small bowl. Spread the mixture on the crackers and grill for 3–4 minutes until browned. Serve hot or warm.

Burlington Croûtes

MAKES 12

100 g/4 oz cooked chicken, finely chopped
30 ml/2 tbsp mayonnaise
2 tomatoes, each cut into 6 thin slices
salt and pepper
12 rounds of fried bread or crackers
butter (optional)
12 stuffed olives

Mix the chicken with the mayonnaise in a bowl. Sprinkle the tomato slices with salt and pepper. If using fried bread, drain thoroughly on absorbent kitchen paper. Butter the crackers, if using.

Place a slice of tomato on each fried bread round or cracker. Pile the chicken mixture on top. Top each croûte with a stuffed olive.

ALTERNATIVE TOPPINGS

A variety of ingredients may be used to top the Burlington Croûtes instead of chicken.

• Drained canned tuna or salmon may be mixed with the mayonnaise.

• Flaked smoked mackerel or chopped pickled herrings may be mixed with soured cream instead of mayonnaise, and a little chopped fresh dill can be added.

• Chopped hard-boiled egg or finely diced cooked ham may be mixed with mayonnaise or with low-fat soft cheese.

Anchovy Appetizers

MAKES 12

fat for greasing
75 g/3 oz plain flour
40 g/1½ oz butter or margarine
1 egg yolk
few drops of anchovy essence
flour for rolling out
ANCHOVY CREAM
1 (50 g/2 oz) can anchovy fillets, drained
1 egg, hard-boiled (yolk only)
25 g/1 oz butter, softened
pinch of cayenne pepper
45 ml/3 tbsp double cream
few drops of red food colouring

Grease two baking sheets. Set the oven at 200°C/400°F/gas 6.

Sift the flour into a mixing bowl and rub in the butter or margarine until the mixture resembles fine breadcrumbs. Add the egg yolk, anchovy essence and enough water to mix to a stiff dough. Roll out thinly on a lightly floured surface and cut into rounds about 2.5–4 cm/1–1½ inches in diameter.

Place on the prepared baking sheets and bake for about 12 minutes until crisp. Cool the biscuits for a few minutes on the baking sheets, then transfer to wire racks to cool completely.

Make the anchovy cream. Put the anchovies in a bowl and pound with the yolk of the hard-boiled egg and the butter until smooth, adding a little cayenne for seasoning. In a second bowl, whip the cream until fairly stiff, then fold it into the anchovy mixture. Add the colouring until the mixture is pale pink. Transfer it to a piping bag fitted with a star nozzle and pipe rosettes of anchovy cream on to the biscuits.

Cheese Butterflies

MAKES 12–18

fat for greasing
100 g/4 oz plain flour
pinch of mustard powder
pinch of salt
pinch of cayenne pepper
75 g/3 oz butter
75 g/3 oz grated Parmesan cheese
1 egg yolk
flour for rolling out
TOPPING
100 g/4 oz cream cheese
few drops of anchovy essence
few drops of red food colouring

Grease two baking sheets. Set the oven at 200°C/400°F/gas 6.

Sift the flour, mustard, salt and cayenne into a bowl. In a mixing bowl, cream the butter until soft and white, then add the flour mixture with the Parmesan. Stir in the egg yolk and enough cold water to form a stiff dough.

Roll out on a lightly floured surface to a thickness of about 3 mm/⅛ inch and cut into rounds about 6 cm/2½ inches in diameter. Cut half the rounds across the centre to make 'wings'.

With a palette knife, lift both the whole rounds and the 'wings' on to the prepared baking sheets and bake for 10 minutes. Cool on the baking sheets.

Meanwhile make the topping. Put the cream cheese in a bowl and cream until soft with a fork, adding the anchovy essence for flavour and just enough of the red food colouring to tint the mixture a pale pink. Transfer the topping to a piping bag fitted with a shell nozzle.

When the biscuits are quite cold, pipe a line of cheese across the centre of each full round and press the straight edges of two half-rounds into the cheese to make them stand up like wings.

Cheese Straws

MAKES 48–60

fat for greasing
100 g/4 oz plain flour
pinch of mustard powder
pinch of salt
pinch of cayenne pepper
75 g/3 oz butter
75 g/3 oz grated Parmesan cheese
1 egg yolk
flour for rolling out

Grease four baking sheets. Set the oven at 200°C/400°F/gas 6.

Make the dough as for Cheese Butterflies (left). Roll it out on a lightly floured surface to a thickness of about 5 mm/¼ inch and cut into fingers, each measuring about 10 x 1 cm/4 inches x ½ inch. From the pastry trimmings make several rings, each about 4 cm/1½ inches in diameter.

With a palette knife, transfer both rings and straws to the prepared baking sheets and bake for 8–10 minutes or until lightly browned and crisp. Cool on the baking sheets.

To serve, fit a few straws through each ring and lay the bundles in the centre of a plate with any remaining straws criss-crossed around them.

SAVOURY BISCUIT SELECTION

*Tempting savoury biscuits are always acceptable with drinks and with decorative presentation
they are perfect for elegant cocktail gatherings.*

*R*efreshments that are easily eaten without using a fork are perfect for informal parties. Be sure to make plenty as guests will keep coming back for more.

Menu for Twelve

SARDINE CASSOLETTES
ONION TRAY BAKE SQUARES
CHICKEN LIVER PATTIES
FILO PASTRIES
BACON ROLLS (PAGE 24)
. . . . .
MINCE PIES (PAGE 56)
GANACHE TRUFFLES
JAM TARTS
. . . . .
MULLED WINE
ALCOHOL-FREE PUNCH

Finger food is practical and popular for informal parties or gatherings. Judging how much to cook can be tricky, but as a general rule guests will eat more of this type of food than of complete meals, such as salads and dishes that are eaten with a fork. Prepare double quantities of the Sardine Cassolettes, Onion Tray Bake and Chicken Liver Patties. Platters of simple sandwiches may be added to the menu, and are a particularly good idea for family parties that include children. Crisply grilled sausages are also popular with children. Place bowls of bought snacks, such as nuts and breadsticks, around the room.

The Onion Tray Bake and Chicken Liver Patties can be made a week or so in advance and frozen, then heated briefly in a hot oven to crisp the pastry before serving. The filo pastries are best frozen uncooked, then baked on the day of the party. The bases for the cassolettes must be prepared on the day they are eaten.

SWEET TREATS

Sweet foods are often ignored in this type of menu, but so many people enjoy them that it is worth including mince pies at Christmas time. Truffles are also extremely popular and the basic ganache recipe can be varied by adding different liqueurs instead of using plain vanilla essence as the flavouring.

For a complete change from these typical festive offerings, or at other times of the year, try including a tray of perfect little jam tarts, filled with a choice of jam or lemon curd, and some topped with a small dollop of clotted cream. Just watch guests' eyes light up at the sight of such an unexpected childhood treat!

QUANTITIES

There is information on preparing food in quantity at the front of the book. Finger food is easy to prepare in large quantities – it simply involves several batch baking sessions. Canapés are more difficult and time consuming to make when entertaining over twenty guests.

When planning a gathering, it is worth remembering that the amount of food consumed will vary according to the time of day and style of party. When a group of friends or family spend a lively informal evening together, everyone will usually eat far more finger food than they would at a formal drinks gathering, or at a short pre-luncheon party. So if you expect the party to stretch from early evening through to midnight, or from lunch time through the afternoon, make sure you have back-up supplies of food for a second wave of snacks.

Sardine Cassolettes

Double the quantities when serving 12.

MAKES 8–10

3 large slices of stale bread, each about 2 cm/¾ inch thick
oil for shallow frying
1 (65 g/2 oz) can sardines in oil, drained
15 ml/1 tbsp Greek yogurt
15 ml/1 tbsp tomato purée
salt and pepper
few drops of lemon juice
10 ml/2 tsp grated Parmesan cheese
watercress sprigs to garnish

Set the oven at 180°C/350°F/gas 4. Using a 5 cm/2 inch biscuit cutter, stamp out 8–10 rounds from the bread. Mark an inner circle on each bread round, using a 4 cm/1½ inch cutter.

Heat the oil in a large frying pan, add the bread rounds and fry until lightly browned on both sides, turning once. Remove the rounds with a slotted spoon and drain on absorbent kitchen paper. With the point of a knife, lift out the inner ring on each round to form a hollow case. Put the cases on a baking sheet and place in the oven for a few minutes to crisp the insides. Cool completely.

Make the filling by mashing the sardines thoroughly and mixing them with the yogurt and tomato purée. Add salt and pepper to taste and stir in the lemon juice and Parmesan. Spoon into the prepared cases and garnish with watercress.

Onion Tray Bake

Make two bakes – 36 squares – for the finger buffet.

MAKES ABOUT 18 SQUARES

fat for greasing
450 g/1 lb strong white flour
5 ml/1 tsp salt
1 sachet fast-action easy-blend yeast
30 ml/2 tbsp olive oil
flour for rolling out
TOPPING
25 g/1 oz butter
450 g/1 lb onions, thinly sliced
15 ml/1 tbsp caraway seeds
salt and pepper
225 g/8 oz quark or curd cheese

Grease a 33 x 23 cm/13 x 9 inch oblong baking tin. Sift the flour and salt into a bowl, then stir in the yeast and make a well in the middle. Add 300 ml/½ pint hand-hot water and the oil; gradually mix the flour into the liquid to make a firm dough.

Turn out the dough on to a lightly floured surface and knead thoroughly until smooth and elastic – about 10 minutes. Then roll out the dough and press it into the tin. Cover loosely with cling film and set aside.

To make the topping, melt the butter in a large frying pan and cook the onions and caraway seeds, stirring often, for about 10 minutes, until the onions have softened slightly. Add salt and pepper to taste, then set aside.

Set the oven at 220°C/425°F/gas 7. Spread the quark or curd cheese over the dough. Top with the onions, spreading them in an even layer and pressing down lightly. Cover loosely with cling film and leave in a warm place for about 15 minutes until slightly risen.

Bake for about 30 minutes, until golden brown. Allow the bake to stand for 5–10 minutes before cutting into squares to serve. Alternatively, the tray bake may be left until just warm or served cold.

Filo Pastries

The basic recipe below is for a Greek speciality: filo triangles with a feta cheese filling. More fillings follow, together with suggestions for shaping the dough in different ways.

MAKES 36

225 g/8 oz feta cheese
5 ml/1 tsp dried oregano
1 spring onion, chopped
pepper
4 sheets of filo pastry
50 g/2 oz butter, melted

Set the oven at 190°C/375°F/gas 5. Mash the feta with the oregano in a bowl, then mix in the spring onion and pepper to taste.

Lay a sheet of filo pastry on a clean, dry surface and brush it with melted butter. Cut the sheet widthways into 9 strips. Keeping the rest of the filo covered while you work, place a little feta mixture at one end of the first strip, leaving the corner of the pastry without filling. Fold the corner diagonally over the feta to cover it in a triangular shape, then fold the mixture over and over to wrap it in several layers of pastry, making a small triangular-shaped pasty.

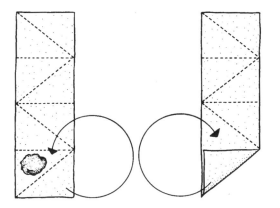

Repeat with the other strips of pastry. Cut and fill the remaining sheets in the same way to make 36 triangular pastries. Place these on baking sheets and brush any remaining butter over them.

Bake for about 10 minutes, until the filo pastry is crisp and golden. Transfer the triangles to a wire rack to cool. They are best served warm.

ALTERNATIVE FILLINGS

Spinach and Cheese Thoroughly drained cooked spinach may be used with or without the cheese. Flavour plain spinach with chopped spring onion and grated nutmeg.

Sardine Mashed canned sardines in tomato sauce make a good filling for filo triangles.

Chicken or Ham Chopped cooked chicken or ham are both tasty fillings for filo. Combine them with a little low-fat soft cheese.

Apricot Apricot halves (drained canned or fresh) topped with a dot of marmalade make good sweet filo pastries. Dust them with icing sugar after baking.

Apple and Almond Mix some ground almonds into cold, sweetened apple purée. Use to fill triangles or squares.

ALTERNATIVE SHAPES

Instead of cutting strips, the pastry may be cut into squares (about six per sheet). The filling should be placed in the middle of the squares, and the pastry gathered up to form small bundles. The butter coating will keep each bundle closed when the filo is pressed together. For strength, the filo may be used double.

Alternatively, squares of filo may be filled and folded into neat oblong parcels. Oblong pieces of filo (about four per sheet) may be folded into neat squares.

FILO PASTRIES

Bought filo pastry is quickly folded around fillings to make stylish savoury snacks for finger-food buffets.

Chicken Liver Patties

MAKES 24

50 g/2 oz butter
1 small onion, chopped
2 rindless bacon rashers, chopped
6 fresh sage leaves or 5 ml/1 tsp dried sage
1 bay leaf
225 g/8 oz chicken livers, trimmed and chopped
4 button mushrooms, chopped
30 ml/2 tbsp plain flour
100 ml/3½ fl oz chicken stock
salt and pepper
15 ml/1 tbsp marsala or sherry
350 g/12 oz puff pastry, thawed if frozen
beaten egg to glaze

Melt half the butter in a saucepan. Add the onion, bacon, sage and bay leaf and fry for about 6 minutes until the onion is softened and the bacon is lightly cooked. Stir in the chopped livers and mushrooms and cook for about 5 minutes more, stirring the mixture occasionally.

Meanwhile, in a second pan, melt the remaining butter, stir in the flour and cook for 1 minute. Gradually add the stock, stirring until the mixture boils and thickens. Stir in the chicken liver mixture with the marsala or sherry and add plenty of salt and pepper. Remove the bay leaf and set the mixture aside to cool.

Set the oven at 190°C/375°F/gas 5. Roll out the pastry thinly on a lightly floured surface, cut out 24 rounds and use to line patty tins. Re-rolling the trimmings, if necessary, cut out 24 slightly smaller rounds for lids. Spoon the liver mixture into the lined tins. Brush the edges of the pastry lids with some of the beaten egg for glazing and press them on the patties, egg-brushed edge down. Press the lids on well. Brush the patties with beaten egg, prick their lids and bake for about 20 minutes. Serve hot or cold.

Ganache Truffles

Ganache is a rich chocolate cream, made by melting chocolate with cream. The chocolate cream may be whipped before it is firm to make a rich topping for cakes; for truffles the mixture is chilled until it is firm.

MAKES ABOUT 25

350 g/12 oz plain chocolate
300 ml/½ pint double cream
5 ml/1 tsp natural vanilla essence
15 ml/1 tbsp icing sugar
cocoa for coating

Break the chocolate into squares and place them in a small saucepan. Add the cream and heat gently, stirring often, until the chocolate melts. Remove from the heat and stir in the vanilla, then allow the mixture to cool, stirring occasionally.

Chill the mixture until it is firm enough to shape. Place the cocoa in a small bowl. Use two teaspoons to shape small balls of mixture and drop them in the cocoa one at a time. Turn the truffles in the cocoa to coat them completely, then place them on a plate or baking sheet and chill again until firm.

Jam Tarts

MAKES 24

225 g/8 oz plain flour
75 g/3 oz butter
50 g/2 oz lard or white vegetable fat
45 g/1½ oz caster sugar
1 egg yolk
5 ml/1 tsp natural vanilla essence
about 120 ml/8 tbsp jam or lemon curd

Sift the flour into a bowl, then rub in the butter and lard or white vegetable fat. Stir in the caster sugar. Lightly whisk the egg yolk with the vanilla essence and 15 ml/1 tbsp water, then use this to bind the dry ingredients into a short dough.

Roll out the pastry and cut out circles to line patty tins. Prink the pastry cases and place a little jam or lemon curd in each. Chill for at least 15 minutes.

Meanwhile, set the oven at 200°C/400°F/gas 6. Bake the tarts for 10–15 minutes, until the pastry is cooked and browned around the edges. Transfer the tarts to a wire rack to cool.

Mulled Wine

This traditional Christmas drink used to be heated by means of a red-hot mulling poker. Today the mixture is more likely to be made on top of the stove, but it remains a welcome warmer on a cold winter's night.

SERVES 12–16

100 g/4 oz caster sugar
1 cinnamon stick
4 cloves
1 nutmeg
3 oranges, thinly sliced
2 bottles red wine

Boil 600 ml/1 pint water with the sugar and spices in a saucepan for 5 minutes. Add the oranges, remove the pan from the heat and set aside for 15 minutes.

Stir in the wine. Heat slowly without boiling. Serve very hot, in heated glasses.

MULLED CIDER

Medium-sweet cider sheds its mundane image when mulled with sweet spices and it is a slightly less alcoholic drink than mulled wine. A bowl of mulled cider made following the recipe above, and simply substituting cider for the wine, can be pepped up by adding a generous tot of brandy.

Alcohol-free Punch

SERVES ABOUT 12

75 g/3 oz caster sugar
50 ml/2 fl oz strong black tea
50 ml/2 fl oz lemon juice
100 ml/3½ fl oz orange juice
300 ml/½ pint white grape juice
½ (227 g/8 oz) can crushed pineapple
450 ml/¾ pint ginger ale
ice cubes
12 maraschino cherries, drained
1 lemon and 1 orange, sliced

Put the sugar in a large saucepan with 900 ml/1½ pints water. Stir over gentle heat until the sugar has dissolved, then boil for 6 minutes. Stir in the tea and set aside until cool. Pour into one or two large jugs or bowls; cover and chill.

When quite cold, add the fruit juices and crushed pineapple. Just before serving, pour in the ginger ale and add the ice cubes. Add the maraschino cherries, stir once and serve with the citrus slices floating on top.

OTHER ALCOHOL-FREE DRINKS

There are lots of commercial alternatives to alcohol, including sparkling mineral waters flavoured with herbs, aromatics and fruit, and fruit juices diluted with water. For a warming winter alternative to mulled wine, try mulling a carton of cranberry juice drink or unsweetened apple juice.

Seafood and champagne make every occasion – and any time of day – extra special. Serve this splendid combination for a late breakfast, early lunch or glamorous supper party.

Menu for Six

GRAVAD LAX
POTTED SHRIMPS OR PRAWNS
CHICKEN OR TURKEY MOUSSE
.....
PEPPER SALAD (PAGE 86)
COURGETTE AND AVOCADO
SALAD
.....
RYE BREAD AND BUTTER
.....
EXOTIC FRUIT BASKET
.....
CHILLED CHAMPAGNE OR
SPARKLING WINE

This menu makes a perfect light lunch or supper and it can be simplified or extended very easily. For a stylish breakfast gathering, double the quantities of Gravad Lax and Potted Prawns or Shrimps and serve them very simply, with the Courgette and Avocado Salad, plenty of rye bread, hot toast fingers and chilled champagne. Chicken or Turkey Mousse and Pepper Salad bring variety to the meal, which can be made more substantial by adding a bowl of potato salad or hot, freshly cooked salad potatoes dressed with melted butter and chopped dill.

Preparations need to begin several days ahead when making Gravad Lax, a form of pickled salmon. Order the salmon in advance and explain that you intend to pickle it, so it must be as fresh as possible. Make a point of asking for the fish to be scaled before it is cleaned and filleted. The pickling process is simple, but it is important to keep the fish in the coolest part of the refrigerator and to turn and baste it with the pickling mixture. The pickling process takes 3 days, but this can be extended for at least another 2 days. Once the fish is drained of the liquid and scraped clean of the pickling mixture it should be eaten within 1–2 days.

EXOTIC FRUIT BASKET

An arrangement of exotic fruit makes an attractive centrepiece for the table as well as offering a fragrant finale for the meal. Here are suggestions for some exotic fruits that taste as exciting as they look.

Persimmons These resemble tomatoes in size and shape, with a large calyx which is usually crisp and dry on top. The skin is edible and the sweet flesh of many varieties, including those known as Sharon fruit, is free from seeds. To serve, cut off the calyx and cut the fruit into wedges. It can eaten with fingers or a fork.

Physalis Sometimes known as Cape gooseberries. Small papery lantern-shaped covers conceal golden-yellow berries. If the fruits are pale, lemon-yellow in colour they are under-ripe and bitter, but they have a sweet, tangy flavour when ripe. Do not strip the fruit before serving; instead, invite guests to open a papery lantern and fold it back, then bite the fruit off its stalk.

Mango There are several varieties. Hard under-ripe fruit is weak in flavour and sharp; fruit that is red, firm and ripe has a pleasing tang to its sweet flavour. Peel the fruit and slice the flesh off the large flat stone.

Passion Fruit Small round and dark coloured, these may be wrinkled or smooth. Cut them in half to reveal crunchy edible seeds and fragrant purple-pink or golden juices. Supply teaspoons so that guests can scoop out the seeds and juices.

Fresh Dates Sweet and firm with papery skins which slide off easily, these can be slit and the stone slipped out for ease of eating.

Gravad Lax

SERVES 6

2 pieces unskinned salmon fillet, total weight about
1 kg/2¼ lb, scaled
200 g/7 oz salt
90 g/3½ oz caster sugar
50 g/2 oz white peppercorns, crushed
90 g/3½ oz fresh dill, plus extra to garnish
MUSTARD SAUCE
30 ml/2 tbsp Swedish mustard (or other mild mustard)
10 ml/2 tsp caster sugar
15 ml/1 tbsp chopped fresh dill
45–60 ml/3–4 tbsp sunflower oil
lemon juice to taste
salt and pepper

Score the skin on each salmon fillet in 4 places. Mix the salt, sugar and peppercorns in a bowl.

Sprinkle a third of the salt mixture on the base of a shallow dish. Place one salmon fillet, skin side down, on the mixture. Cover with a further third of the salt mixture and add half the dill. Arrange the second fillet, skin side up, on top. Cover with the remaining salt mixture and dill.

Cover with foil. Place a plate or oblong baking sheet or tin on top of the fish and weight it down. Leave in the refrigerator for 36 hours, during which time the salt mixture will become a brine solution. Turn the whole fillet 'sandwich' every day and baste with the liquor.

For the sauce, mix the mustard, sugar and dill. Add the oil very slowly, beating all the time to make a thick sauce. Stir in a little lemon juice with salt and pepper to taste.

Drain off the brine from the fish and scrape away the dill and peppercorns before serving. Serve thinly sliced, garnished with fresh dill. Offer the mustard sauce separately.

Potted Shrimps or Prawns

MAKES ABOUT 675 G/1½ LB

225 g/8 oz unsalted butter
450 g/1 lb peeled cooked shrimps or prawns
1.25 ml/¼ tsp ground white pepper
1.25 ml/¼ tsp ground mace
1.25 ml/¼ tsp ground cloves
dill sprigs to garnish

Melt the butter in a saucepan, add the shrimps or prawns and heat very gently, without boiling. Add the pepper, mace and cloves. Using a slotted spoon, transfer the shrimps or prawns to small pots. Pour a little of the hot spiced butter into each pot.

Set the remaining spiced butter aside until the residue has settled, then pour over the shrimps or prawns. Chill until the butter is firm. Store in a refrigerator for no more than 48 hours. Garnish with dill. Serve with rye bread or fingers of hot toast.

POTTED CRAB
Crab meat can be potted in the same way as shrimps or prawns to make a delicious savoury spread. Buy fresh dressed crab (substitute 2 medium crabs for the prawns in the above recipe) or use frozen crabmeat (thawed) instead of the prawns. Break up the white meat with a fork and mix it with the brown meat before adding it to the spiced butter. Continue as above.

Chicken or Turkey Mousse

SERVES 4–6

225 g/8 oz cooked chicken or turkey breast meat
275 ml/9 fl oz double cream
275 ml/9 fl oz chicken stock with fat removed
15 ml/1 tbsp gelatine
3 egg yolks, beaten
salt and pepper
20 ml/4 tsp mayonnaise
GARNISH
watercress sprigs
small lettuce leaves

Remove any skin, gristle and fat from the poultry, mince it finely and put it in a bowl. In a second bowl, whip the cream lightly. Chill until required. Place a mixing bowl in the refrigerator to chill.

Put 100 ml/3½ fl oz of the stock in a heatproof bowl, sprinkle on the gelatine and set aside for 15 minutes until spongy. Put the rest of the stock in the top of a double saucepan and stir in the beaten egg yolks, with salt and pepper.

Place the pan over simmering water and cook gently, stirring frequently, until the mixture thickens slightly. Remove from the heat and pour into the chilled bowl. Stand the bowl containing the gelatine over a saucepan of hot water and stir until the gelatine has dissolved completely. Stir into the egg mixture, mixing well. Add the minced chicken or turkey and stir until thoroughly mixed.

Stand the bowl in a basin of cold water or crushed ice, or place in the refrigerator until the mousse mixture begins to thicken at the edges. Fold in the chilled whipped cream and the mayonnaise. Turn into a wetted 1 litre/1¾ pint mould and chill until set. To serve, turn out on to a platter and garnish with the watercress and lettuce leaves.

Courgette and Avocado Salad

SERVES 6

salt and pepper
450 g/1 lb courgettes, thickly sliced
1 Lollo Rosso lettuce, separated into leaves
2 avocados
3 rindless streaky bacon rashers, grilled, to garnish
DRESSING
75 ml/5 tbsp olive oil
30 ml/2 tbsp tarragon or white wine vinegar
pinch of caster sugar
1 garlic clove, crushed
salt and pepper

Make the dressing by mixing all the ingredients in a screw-topped jar. Close the jar tightly and shake vigorously until well blended.

Bring a saucepan of salted water to the boil, add the courgettes, bring the water back to the boil, then drain the courgettes and put them in a bowl. While still warm, pour the dressing over. Allow the mixture to cool, then cover and marinate in the refrigerator for 2–3 hours.

Wash the Lollo Rosso leaves and dry them thoroughly. Shred the leaves into a salad bowl. Drain the courgettes, reserving the dressing, and spoon on top of the Lollo Rosso.

Peel and slice the avocados, toss them lightly in the reserved dressing, then arrange on top of the salad, using a slotted spoon. Crumble a little bacon over the salad. Serve at once with the remaining dressing in a small jug.

GRAVAD LAX AND POTTED SHRIMPS OR PRAWNS

*Fine simple foods, served in style, make a menu with real panache – the perfect way to see out the
old year and celebrate the new one.*

Cheese and Wine Revival

*I*t's time to bring back that classic combination: cheese and wine is easy to serve and always popular, especially with the array of international cheeses now available.

Menu for Twelve

MRS BEETON'S PASTRY
RAMAKINS (PAGE 69)
CHEESE BUTTERFLIES AND
CHEESE STRAWS (PAGE 102)
HOT PEPPER CHEESES
.....
HARD CHEESE WITH CELERY
AND APPLES
SEMI-SOFT CHEESE WITH
GRAPES
SOFT CHEESE WITH FIGS AND
DATES
.....
CRISP CRACKERS
CHESHIRE CHIPS
CARAWAY CRACKERS
OATCAKES

Prepare cheese savouries to hand around when guests first arrive, then invite them to help themselves from a buffet of cheese platters. French bread may be offered as well as the crackers if liked.

Buy large pieces of cheese instead of a lot of small portions as they look more inviting and there is proportionally less waste from small amounts of cheese left on the rind. Place the different types of cheese on separate platters, garnishing each with fruit or celery.

Hard Cheese British favourites include Wensleydale, a good farmhouse Cheddar, Lancashire, Double Gloucester, farmhouse Leicester and Cheshire. Jarlsberg, Gruyère or Emmenthal, Gouda, Leiden (flavoured with caraway) and Tomme de Savoie are typical international examples.

Blue Cheese Select one or two firm British cheeses, such as Stilton, Blue Cheshire, Lanark Blue or Blue Wensleydale. Roquefort, Dolcelatte, Bleu d'Auvergne and Cambazola are international varieties.

Semi-soft Cheeses Brie and Camembert are the most popular choice. There are many varieties of these famous cheeses, so you can offer several. Other semi-soft cheeses include Coulommiers, Munster, Pont l'Evêque, Saint Paulin and Reblochon.

Soft Cheeses Although these are more often used for cooking, including one or two soft cheeses on the buffet table is a good idea as they are delicious with dates or figs. Surround dishes of ricotta and mascarpone with fruit, celery and small water biscuits.

Goats' and Ewes' Cheese Keep these separate from the cows' milk cheeses as they have a strong, distinctive flavour which is not to everyone's taste. Chèvre or Bouche de Chèvre is a cylindrical French soft rind cheese with a white bloom. There are several British soft cheeses in rounds, cylinders or pyramid shapes. Among the many firm or hard goats' and ewes' cheeses are Ribblesdale and Sheviok.

Hot Pepper Cheeses

When freshly cooked, these savouries are inclined to crumble and break easily. For this reason it is best to allow them to cool completely, then reheat gently until just warm.

MAKES 40–50

fat for greasing
200 g/7 oz plain flour
200 g/7 oz butter
200 g/7 oz Lancashire cheese, grated
few drops of hot pepper sauce
1.25 ml/¼ tsp salt
flour for rolling out

Grease four baking sheets. Sift the flour into a mixing bowl. Rub in the butter until the mixture resembles fine breadcrumbs. Add the cheese, hot pepper sauce and salt. Work the mixture thoroughly by hand to make a smooth dough. Use a few drops of water if necessary, but the dough will be shorter and richer without it. Chill for 30 minutes.

Meanwhile, set the oven at 180°C/350°F/gas 4. Roll out the dough on a floured surface to a thickness of 5 mm/¼ inch. Cut into rounds or shapes.

With a palette knife, transfer the shapes to the prepared baking sheets and bake for 10–12 minutes or until lightly browned and crisp. Cool on the baking sheets.

CUTTING THE DOUGH

When cutting out the cheese dough it is best to stick to regular shapes such as rounds, crescents, squares or stars. The mixture is so short that any thin projections on the biscuits are likely to break off.

Crisp Crackers

These plain crackers are the ideal accompaniment for cheese. If you use very small cutters for the dough, the crackers can be used as a base for bite-sized canapés – top them with piped smooth pâté or cream cheese, olives and parsley.

MAKES ABOUT 24

fat for greasing
225 g/8 oz plain flour
2.5 ml/½ tsp salt
about 125 ml/4 fl oz milk
1 egg yolk, beaten

Grease two baking sheets. Set the oven at 180°C/350°F/gas 4. Sift the flour and salt into a bowl. Make a well in the middle and add about half the milk with the egg yolk. Gradually work in the flour to make a firm dough, adding more milk as necessary.

Turn the dough out on to a lightly floured surface and knead it briefly until it is perfectly smooth. Divide the piece of dough in half and wrap one piece in cling film to prevent it from drying out while you roll out the other piece.

Roll out the dough very thinly and use a 7.5 cm/3 inch round cutter to stamp out crackers. Gather up the trimmings and re-roll them. Place the crackers on the prepared baking sheets and bake them for 12–18 minutes, until they are golden. Transfer the crackers to a wire rack to cool.

Caraway Crackers

MAKES ABOUT 30

fat for greasing
50 g/2 oz butter, softened
225 g/8 oz plain flour
30 ml/2 tbsp caraway seeds
good pinch of salt
1 egg, beaten
milk for glazing

Grease two baking sheets. Set the oven at 180°C/350°F/gas 4. Place the butter in a small bowl and beat it until it is very soft. Gradually beat in the flour, caraway seeds and salt until the ingredients are thoroughly mixed.

Add the beaten egg and mix well to make a firm dough. Knead the dough briefly on a floured surface, then roll it out thinly and cut out 5 cm/2 inch circles.

Place the crackers on the baking sheets. Brush them with a little milk, then bake for 12–15 minutes. Transfer the crackers to a wire rack to cool.

Cheshire Chips

MAKES 50-60

fat for greasing
50 g/2 oz plain flour
50 g/2 oz butter
50 g/2 oz Cheshire cheese, grated
50 g/2 oz fresh white breadcrumbs
1.25 ml/¼ tsp cayenne pepper
1.25 ml/¼ tsp salt
flour for rolling out

Grease four baking sheets. Sift the flour into a mixing bowl. Rub in the butter until the mixture resembles fine breadcrumbs. Add the cheese, breadcrumbs and seasonings. Work the mixture thoroughly by hand to make a smooth dough. Chill for 30 minutes.

Meanwhile, set the oven at 180°C/350°F/gas 4. Roll out the dough on a floured surface to a thickness of 5 mm/¼ inch. Cut into thin chips, each measuring about 3 mm x 5 cm/⅛ inch x 2 inches.

With a palette knife, transfer the chips to the prepared baking sheets and bake for 7–10 minutes or until lightly browned and crisp. Cool on the baking sheets.

Oatcakes

MAKES ABOUT 16

fat for greasing
25 g/1 oz bacon fat or dripping
225 g/8 oz medium oatmeal
1.25 ml/¼ tsp salt
1.25 ml/¼ tsp bicarbonate of soda
fine oatmeal for rolling out

Grease two baking sheets. Set the oven at 160°C/325°F/gas 3.

Melt the bacon fat or dripping in a large saucepan. Remove from the heat and stir in the dry ingredients, then gradually add 60–75 ml/4–5 tbsp boiling water, stirring it in to make a stiff dough.

Cool slightly, then knead the dough together and cut it in half. Knead a portion of dough well and roll it out on a surface dusted with fine oatmeal or flour to a circle measuring about 18 cm/7 inches in diameter. Cut into wedges and transfer to the prepared baking sheet.

Repeat with the remaining dough. Bake the oatcakes for 20–30 minutes. Cool on a wire rack.

HOME-MADE SAVOURY CRACKERS

Offer only the best by baking a selection of simple savoury crackers to complement fine cheese and wine.

Selecting Wine for a Special Meal

*W*hen much effort is spent planning and preparing food, an interesting and appropriate choice *of wine adds the perfect finishing touch to a special menu. Even though the excellent variety of wines in larger supermarkets is matched by background information, helpful comments and quality or taste ratings, deciding on the ideal bottle can be mind-boggling, especially when dinner is only a few hours ahead.*

Tradition usually demands that like matches like: a delicate dish goes with a light, elegant wine, while a full-flavoured dish requires a full-bodied, robust wine. Modern experiments have almost proved the contrary, that a rich, creamy dish can be accompanied by a light, slightly tart, completely contrasting wine, or a plain roasted fowl can provide the background to a massively proportioned one. Both schools would agree that regional dishes are at their best with local wines, that food cooked in wine should be enjoyed with a wine of the same origin (preferably superior) and that, although they are deemed perfect partners, cheese tends to benefit more from the accompaniment of wine than vice-versa. Wine is usually selected to complement food; however, if one or several particular wines are to be drunk for their own sake as a focal point for the meal, the menu must be planned around the wines.

Aperitifs Classic aperitifs are dry (usually *brut*) Champagne, Fino or Manzanilla sherry or a dry white wine. To these may be added fuller-bodied sherries (Amontillado, dry Oloroso), dry Madeiras, the drier versions of fortified wines made from red grapes (Banyuls, Tawny Port) and the sweet fortified wines from white grapes (Muscat de Beaumes-de-Venise *et al*). Sweet sherries are not suitable. The French habit of serving dessert wines as an aperitif has much to recommend it.

First Courses Wine is not usually served with soup, although sherry or Madeira may be. If a sturdy soup plays a large part in a meal then a straight-forward wine, white or red of matching flavour, should be served. Such soups are generally highly flavoured, and would overwhelm a fine wine. A dry white wine or a light, young red is a good choice for many starters and appetizers.

However, rich pâtés and terrines should be accompanied by an accordingly fuller wine, or one with more personality. The fattiness in cold meats requires a level of acidity (in white wines) or youthful tannin (in red wines) that also excludes the best from the cellar.

Fish and Seafood Most fish goes well with white wine, and the more complex the preparation, the more interesting the wine should be; however, a plain grilled fish can be served with the grandest of white wines. Richly fleshed fish (turbot, bass, salmon) need wines of flavour and structure, and salmon can often be accompanied by a red wine that is low in tannin, such as a Pinot Noir, and if it is cooked in red wine, it must be accompanied by red wine.

Oysters are generally accompanied by dry white wines, which should be crisp, clean and not too exuberantly fruity (Gewürztraminer would be impossible with any mollusc). In Andalusia, Manzanilla or Fino sherry is served with shellfish. Most larger crustaceans (lobster, crayfish) are both costly and flavourful, and should go with a fuller, more complex white wine, even one with a certain age.

Poultry Chicken is the perfect dish for almost any wine – white, red or rosé. A plain roast chicken is as at home with a Chardonnay, Gamay, Cabernet, Pinot Noir, even Syrah if the bird is roasted with a few herbs. The more highly sauced the dish, the more robust should be the wine. Duck requires red wine, and the fattiness of an Aylesbury duck is well matched by red wines from the Loire and Rhône Valleys (or their international equivalents), while a wild duck needs a firmer Cabernet or Merlot.

White Meats and Offal These can be served with white or red wines, but the white must have a certain body and fruit. Unless the dishes are heavily spiced, a delicate red such as Chinon (Cabernet Franc) or Côte de Beaune (Pinot Noir) is perfect.

Red Meats Beef, lamb, venison and wild boar all cry out for red wines. Stews and hotpots go well with less sophisticated wines. Roasts generally require wines of complexity and stature.

Game Here, the choice falls generally on firm, robust reds which would be anything from Bordeaux, Burgundy, the Rhône Valley or northern Italy. Game stews or casseroles do not need the grandest bottles, but properly roasted game is the perfect partner for the best red wine you possess.

Spicy Dishes By the fact of being spicy, such dishes will destroy the finesse of a good wine. A good rosé (not a 'blush' wine) or a young, fruity red not too high in acidity (Australian Shiraz) would do well, and may be served chilled. Gewürztraminer is known to go well with the Asian cuisine.

Cheese A fine cheese has as much regionality about it as a fine wine. Cheeses are often made where wines are not, but where there is a natural marriage – Munster and the wines of Alsace, Epoisses and Burgundy, Crottin de Chavignol and Sancerre, Parmesan and Chianti – this should be followed. For the most part, cheese will follow the main course for which a wine has already been selected; if this course has had a white wine, it could be the opportunity to change to red (although the tannin in many red wines does not help the cheese). Most cheeses are better with white wine, even semi-sweet, than red. Port and Stilton is more of a tradition than a perfect match.

Desserts The majority of dessert dishes smother the flavour of a wine, the exceptions being plain fruit flans, a light gâteau or fresh fruit. The fine natural sweet wines of the world are best drunk on their own, with the dessert acting as the excuse. Fortified wines such as the Muscats will stand up well to anything. Champagne or sparkling wine with dessert or at the end of a meal must be *demi-sec* or *doux*, never *brut*.

Digestifs These are taken after a meal. In this category are all wine-based and fruit-based spirits, brandies and liqueurs.

WHITE WINES

Very Dry White Wines These are wines that are relatively light in colour and relatively high in acidity. Dryness should not, however, be equated with acidity, for all wines have acidity, even the very sweetest: here we are looking at the total absence of sweetness. If the acidity is pronounced, as it is in a Muscadet from France or a Vinho Verde from Portugal, it should be a crisp, mouthwatering acidity, in harmony with the wine's fruit and character; a wine that has too much acidity comes from unripe grapes.

The following well-known wines fit into the very dry category. France: Muscadet, Pouilly-Fumé, Sancerre and most Loire whites, Entre-Deux-Mers, minor Graves, Sylvaner, Bourgogne-Aligoté and Chablis. Italy: Soave, Galestro, Orvieto secco, Verdicchio and most wines made with Chardonnay, Pinot Grigio or Sauvignon grapes. Germany: all wines with *trocken* on the label. Spain: most young wines from Rioja and the Penedès. The New World: most Sauvignons, unless they specify 'late harvest' on the label, dry Chenin Blancs, very few Chardonnays.

Wines in this category are generally drunk young, in the year following the vintage, for often the main pleasure lies in their youthful freshness which is lost if kept for too long. Many are at their best served as an aperitif, but all will go well with food.

Dry White Wines This category covers the majority of white wines for drinking with food. They will have very little or no residual sugar after fermentation, and are therefore dry, but are fuller bodied than the very dry white wines. This is evident in the richer texture (more extract and a slightly higher degree of alcohol), greater complexity and ageing potential.

The following wines fit into the dry white category. France: all white burgundies (Chablis, Meursault, the

Montrachet family, Mâcon blanc, Pouilly-Fuissé), Riesling and Pinot Gris from Alsace, most white wines from the Rhône and Provence, the better Graves from Bordeaux and Loire Valley whites from good vintages. Italy: wines from the Tocai grape, higher-priced Chardonnays, Tuscan whites except Galestro, Greco di Tufo. Spain: wood-aged whites from Rioja and Penedès. Germany: most *halb-trocken* wines from the Mosel or the Rheingau, especially Rieslings. The New World: most Chardonnays, Semillons (Australia) and wood-aged Sauvignons.

Most of these dry wines are drinkable young, right after bottling, but it is not then that they are at their best. The extra levels of alcohol, fruit sugar and extract need time to develop their inherent style and character. When developed they are the perfect accompaniment to a meal.

Aromatic White Wines Wines in this category can be dry, off-dry or sweet, but share a dominance of aroma over flavour, and as such are difficult to fit into a meal. The classical wine regions, apart from Alsace, do not look for overtly aromatic wines so these are recognized more by their grape variety. The Muscat or, in Italy, the Moscata grape is intensely aromatic, with a dry or sweet finish according the vinification. With Gewürztraminer, and to a lesser extent Traminer, the aroma generally dominates the often spicy, ripe fruit. Such wines are best drunk relatively young.

Sweet White Wines This category covers wines where the sugar in the grape juice is not fully fermented out into alcohol, leaving a sweet taste. While aromatic wines are not necessarily sweet (the dry Muscats, for example) there are those, particularly the heady Gewürztraminers made from very ripe grapes, that are richly aromatic and finish off-dry. Here, we are looking at wines that are just not off-dry, but range from being semi-sweet to very sweet indeed.

The following wines are all classed as sweet white. France: Sauternes, Barsac and similar wines from the Bordeaux region, Monbazillac, Jurançon, Vouvray *moelleux*, Coteaux du Layon and similar sweet wines from Anjou, some *vendange tardive* and all *sélection de grains nobles* wines from Alsace. Germany: most *spätlese*, all *auslese*, *beerenauslese* and *trockenbeerenauslese* wines, as well as *Eiswein*. Italy: *Vino Santo* and any wines stating *abboccato* or *recioto* on the label, as well as the *DOC Amarone*. The New World: most Chenin Blancs, unless stated to be dry, and all late harvest Sauvignon, Semillon and Riesling.

The degree of sweetness of the *demi-sec* and *moelleux* wines varies with the type of wine and the vintage. Wines that are sweet by definition, like Sauternes, will be sweeter in a year of greater concentration, since the higher lever of natural sugar in the grapes will leave more residual sugar. Wines that are sweet by choice of the winemaker, such as those from Vouvray, Anjou and Alsace, and all late-harvest wines will only appear in years when there is enough over-ripeness in the grapes to produce the desired concentration and richness. Fine sweet wines, however rich, should not be too cloying for they will be balanced by natural acidity. These wines should *look* sweet, just as very dry wines *look* dry. Unlike medium-bodied dry white wines, they are often best drunk on their own.

ROSÉS

Rosé wines are often referred to as 'pink' wines. With the exception of Rosé Champagne, where red wine can be added at the time of *dégorgement*, all rosés derive their colour from a very short maceration of red grapes before the juice is run off. There are very few wines that are specifically rosé – Tavel in the southern Rhône Valley is an example – so the production of rosé and its depth of colour is up to the winemaker. Wrongly viewed as a cross between red and white wine, rosés are an important category in their own right, from the faintly coloured 'blush' wines created in California, to the more full-bodied Rosé de Provence or Rosados from Spain. Generally, rosés should be fresh and appealing, and should be drunk young.

RED WINES

Light Red Wines This category covers wines that are not necessarily light in colour, but are light in body. Such wines may come from young vines, a shorter than usual maceration, vintages lacking in ripeness, or they may be red wines from predominantly white wine regions, Sancerre or the Savoie for example. The warmer the growing region, the less easy it is to make a light red wine. They will almost always be young as lightness means a lack of extraction of tannin and

alcohol in favour of an appealing fruit; therefore, although they may be kept, they do not have much potential for improvement. This category should not be confused with the basic everyday table wines; these are blended for immediate consumption, but are not necessarily light. The best-known wine in this category is Beaujolais, possibly rivalled by Valpolicella. These wines will benefit from being drunk cool, to enhance the fruit.

Medium-bodied Red Wines This category covers most red table wines, which not only have more weight, but also more depth and complexity, thus more potential. Such wines should therefore not be drunk in their first youth, as should the lighter reds.

These wines are classic examples of medium-bodied reds. France: Bordeaux and Burgundy (except the best wines in the best vintages), the Loire Valley, the South West and Provence. Italy: Piedmont, (except Barolo), Tuscany, the Veneto and most wines made with Cabernet, Merlot or Sangiovese grapes. Spain: Rioja, Penedès. Portugal: Dão. The New World: most wines from Cabernet, Merlot and Pinot Noir grapes.

Full-bodied Red Wines Here we are looking at wines that are not merely high in extract and alcohol, but which also possess richness, depth and ageing potential. They will either come from a warm climate, or from robust grape varieties such as Syrah or Mourvedre, and almost always from a good vintage. These are dark-coloured, sturdy wines, not lacking in finesse but with great presence on the palate. They should accompany food which enhances these characteristics rather than allows itself to be smothered by them. These mouth-filling wines are too massive to drink young, except perhaps in the open air. They begin to show well at five to six years, and can last two decades or more.

The best-known full-bodied reds are as follows. France: the richer Pomerols and Saint-Emilions from Bordeaux, some Côte de Nuits burgundies, most red wines from the Rhône Valley and some from Provence and the South West. Italy: Barolo and Gattinara from Piedmont, and wines from southern Italy, especially Taurasi. The New World: almost all wines made from the Zinfandel, Syrah and Mourvèdre grapes, and many from the Cabernet Sauvignon and Merlot.

SPARKLING WINES

Wines can be made sparkling by a variety of methods and they are now made all over the world. The most famous is Champagne. Wines that achieved their sparkle in bottle (as opposed to in a tank or vat) were known as *méthode champenoise*; however the term has now been changed to *méthode traditionelle*. Sparkling wines may be *brut* (very dry), *sec, demi-sec* or *doux* (very sweet), and may be vintage or non-vintage. Non-vintage wines can be drunk immediately, but benefit from a further few months' ageing; vintage wines should be drunk at five to ten years. Generally perfect as an aperitif, the best sparkling wines go very well with a meal.

FORTIFIED WINES

Fortified wines are those to which alcohol, usually grape brandy, has been added during fermentation to arrest this process, thereby leaving a considerable amount of unfermented sugar as well as substantially increasing the alcoholic content. Such wines, therefore, will be both fortified and sweet.

The most famous come from Portugal (port) and Spain (sherry), while other well-known wines are Madeira, Marsala and Malaga. The fortified Muscat de Beaumes-de-Venise, Muscat de Rivesaltes and Banyuls come from France, and similar styles of Muscat and late harvest red grapes such as Zinfandel and Grenache are from the New World. Australia has some particularly successful liqueur Muscats.

Fortified wines are generally drunk on their own, either as an aperitif or after meals. The pale coloured wines, based on white grapes, should be drunk young, as they 'maderize', that is gain colour and lose their freshness with age. The more robust wines based on red grapes, especially wines carrying a vintage date, should be matured in the bottle. Fortified wines carrying the description 'tawny' have been aged in barrel or vat and should be drunk a few months after purchase.

Cocktails and Other Drinks

*I*t is absolutely essential to offer a good choice of sophisticated alcohol-free drinks whenever you entertain, from mineral water with the meal to fruit juices, herb-flavoured sparkling mineral waters or non-alcoholic cocktails according to the occasion. The days of indulging with sheer abandon may well have waned, but there is no need to commit everyone to soft drinks and wine at every party. Pre-dinner cocktails and liqueurs with coffee are still a splendid treat, especially when shared with friends or family who journey no farther than the guest room at the end of the evening.

COCKTAILS

The popularity of the cocktail waxes and wanes, and whether you elect to surprise your guests with a Sidecar or Screwdriver depends very much on the state of your liquor cabinet, the sophistication of your bar equipment and whether anyone is expecting to drive home. Many cocktails taste deceptively innocent, but are in fact highly alcoholic. There are hundreds of different cocktails; a few of the more popular varieties are listed below:

Americano 1 part each of Campari and sweet vermouth, stirred in a tall glass and topped up with soda. Add a slice of orange.

Black Velvet 1 part each of dry Champagne and bitter stout (usually Guiness). Pour simultaneously into a tall jug. Serve in tall glasses or tankards.

Bloody Mary 1 part vodka to 2 parts tomato juice. Serve on crushed ice and stir in Worcestershire sauce, lemon juice, salt and pepper to taste. Tabasco may also be added if liked.

Bronx 3 parts gin to 1 part each of dry vermouth, sweet vermouth and orange juice, shaken, then strained into tall glasses.

Bucks Fizz 1 part orange juice to 2 parts chilled Champagne. Serve in tall glasses; do not add ice.

Champagne Cocktail Put 1 sugar lump into a Champagne flute. Soak in Angostura bitters. Add about 5 ml/1 tsp brandy and top up with chilled Champagne.

Daiquiri 3 parts white rum to 1 part fresh lime or lemon juice. Add 1.25 ml/¼ tsp caster sugar, shake, then strain into cocktail glasses.

Dry Martini 2 parts dry gin to 1 part dry vermouth, stirred in a mixing glass, then strained over cracked ice in a cocktail glass. Serve with a twist of lemon rind.

Horse's Neck Pare the rind of a lemon in a long spiral; hook it over the rim of a tumbler so that it curls over. Anchor the end inside the glass with 2 ice cubes. Add 40 ml/1½ fl oz brandy and fill with ginger ale. Add a few drops of Angostura bitters, if liked.

Kir 1 part Crème de Cassis to 6 parts chilled white Burgundy. Pour the wine over the Cassis in a balloon glass. Ice is optional.

Manhattan 2 parts bourbon to 1 part sweet vermouth. Stir in a mixing glass with a few drops of Angostura bitters, if liked. Serve over cracked ice and top with a maraschino cherry.

Negroni 1 part each of dry gin, sweet vermouth and Campari. Pour over ice cubes in a tall glass and top up with soda water if liked. Add a slice of orange.

Old Fashioned Put 1 sugar lump into a tall glass. Soak in Angostura bitters. Add enough water to dissolve the sugar (about 10 ml/2 tsp). Pour over 75 ml/3 fl oz rye or bourbon. Decorate with a maraschino cherry and an orange slice.

Pink Gin Shake a few drops of Angostura bitters into a wine or cocktail glass. Roll the bitters around the glass. Pour away, if liked. Add 40 ml/1½ fl oz gin to the glass with ice cubes, if liked.

Screwdriver 2 parts orange juice to 1 part vodka. Stir in a wine or cocktail glass. Add ice cubes and decorate with a slice of orange.

Sidecar 2 parts brandy to 1 part each of Cointreau and lemon juice. Shake with cracked ice, then strain into a cocktail glass.

Vodkatini 2 parts vodka to 1 part dry vermouth, stirred together in a mixing glass, then strained into a cocktail glass. Serve with ice and a twist of lemon rind.

Whisky Mac 1 part each of whisky and ginger wine, stirred together in a wine or cocktail glass. Do not add any ice.

GLOSSARY OF SPIRITS AND LIQUEURS

Advocaat A Dutch beverage made of brandy, egg yolks and cream with an alcoholic content of 15–18%.

Alcools Blancs Fruit brandies made in Alsace, the best known being Kirsch, Framboise, Mirabelle, Quetsch and Poire Williams (see individual entries).

Angostura A popular French and Spanish liqueur or aperitif, based on the anise plant, better known in France under the brand names of Pernod and Ricard (see Pastis).

Anisette A liqueur of aniseed flavour. The best-known brand is Marie Brizard.

Apricot Brandy Dry, unsweetened brandy made from the distilled juice of apricots.

Apricot Liqueur A very sweet liqueur, made from the juice of mashed apricots and sweetened brandy.

Aquavit A white spirit, generally of Scandinavian origin, flavoured with certain aromatic seeds and spices, of which caraway seeds are the most popular.

Armagnac Grape brandy from south-west France compared to, but quite different from, Cognac. The best comes from the Bas-Armagnac, followed by Tenareze and Haut-Armagnac. A more fiery spirit than Cognac, Armagnac stands up better to lengthy wood-ageing. Old vintage Armagnac is very sought after.

Arrack A distilled spirit made in eastern Europe, often flavoured with aniseed, also known as Arak and Raki.

Athol Brose A Scottish liqueur based on whisky mixed with honey.

'B and B' Benedictine and brandy, bottled half-and-half.

Bacardi A well-known brand of rum.

Benedictine A liqueur based on brandy, with a variety of herbs, plants and infusions from a recipe originating from the Benedictine monastery at Fecamp.

Bitters Diverse spirits flavoured with herbs and roots, generally sold under brand names (see Angostura, Campari, Fernet Branca).

Black Velvet Dry Champagne and stout, mixed half-and-half.

Bourbon A type of American whiskey, usually from Tennessee.

Brandy Literally distilled wine, the word now covers fruit brandies. Made in most wine-growing countries, brandy should not be confused with Calvados, Grappa or Marc.

Byrrh A popular French quinine-flavoured aperitif.

Calvados Apple brandy, distilled from cider in Normandy, France. The finest is from the Vallée d'Auge. Young, it is very fiery but good for cooking; old, it is very fine.

Campari Italian proprietary bitters of aperitif strength.

Carpano Italian sweet vermouth.

Chambery Town in the Savoie (France) that produces a dry vermouth and also a raspberry-flavoured version called Chamberyzette.

Chartreuse An internationally famous liqueur made by the Carthusian monks both in Spain and France. The green is finer and more spirity; the yellow sweet and less alcoholic.

Cherry Brandy A liqueur derived from cherry juice and brandy, with crushed cherry stones giving it a bitter-almond taste.

Cherry Heering A cherry liqueur made in Copenhagen by the Peter Heering company.

Cognac Brandy made in western France around the town of Cognac from distilled white wine. Cognac is recognized as the finest brandy in the world, and owes its distinction to the soil, methods of distillation and ageing. The Cognac region is strictly controlled, the finest spirit coming from the Grande Champagne and Petite Champagne regions.

Crème Sweet liqueurs, generally made from fruit or other flavourings, which use the word 'crème' to distinguish them from dry brandies, but have nothing to do with cream. The best-known is Crème de Cassis, the blackcurrant liqueur.

Curaçao A style of liqueur made from the skins of

oranges, now sold under brand names such as Cointreau and Grand Marnier. Also seen as Triple Sec.

Cynar An Italian aperitif based on artichokes.

Drambuie A proprietary liqueur made from Scotch Whisky, heather, honey and herbs.

Dubonnet A proprietary French aperitif based on fortified wine flavoured with quinine.

Eau-de-vie The generic French term for distilled wine or fruits.

Fernet Branca Internationally famous Italian bitters, supposedly drunk as an aperitif, but more generally used for upset stomachs or hangovers.

Fine Champagne A Cognac coming from a blend of the produce of Grande Champagne and Petite Champagne.

Framboise French *eau-de-vie* distilled from raspberries.

Geneva Name used in Holland for Dutch gin.

Gentiane A French or Swiss liqueur distilled from the gentian root. The best-known brand is Suze.

Gin A juniper-flavoured white spirit made from distilled grain. British (or London dry) gin is dry, Dutch gin is sweeter, distilled at a lower proof and may be aged.

Grappa The Italian word for 'marc', or any spirit distilled from the 'cake' or pressed skins and pips of grapes after wine-making.

Grog A generic term for a hot drink of spirits, usually rum, diluted with hot water, lemon and spices.

Hollands Dutch gin, known in Holland as Jenever.

Izarra A Chartreuse-style liqueur, made in the Basque country in France in both the green and yellow styles.

Julep An American cold drink, based on Bourbon, sugar, mint and crushed ice.

Kir A French aperitif made by pouring a dry white wine over a dash of liqueur de cassis.

Kirsch White brandy distilled from cherries complete with stones and principally made in Alsace, Germany and Switzerland.

Kummel Spirit from grain alcohol flavoured with caraway seeds, this is sweet and often drunk on the rocks.

Lillet A French wine-based aperitif from Podensac, near Bordeaux.

Mandarine A sweet, orange-coloured liqueur with the flavour of tangerines.

Maraschino A liqueur made from the Mascara cherry.

Marc *Eau-de-vie* made from the maceration with alcohol of the 'cake' of grape skins and pips after the wine has fermented. All wine-producing regions make a marc (see Grappa). It is best if aged for several years in wood.

Mead A beverage made from fermented honey, usually under 10% alcohol and very sweet.

Mirabelle White fruit brandy made from the mirabelle plum. The finest is the Mirabelle de Lorraine.

Ouzo A spirit with an anis base, comparable to Pernod.

Pastis The generic term for a spirit made with herb flavourings, notably anis or liquorice. Pastis is drunk as an aperitif, with water.

Pernod A proprietary brand of pastis.

Pimm's An alcoholic cordial based on gin, rum, brandy and whisky, to be drunk as a long drink with lemonade, borage and ice.

Plymouth Gin Intermediate in style between London gin and Hollands gin.

Poire A white fruit brandy made from the William pear.

Quetsch A white fruit brandy made in Alsace and Lorraine from plums.

Ricard A proprietary brand of pastis, and a rival to Pernod.

Rum A spirit distilled from the products of fermented sugar cane. When distilled, rum is colourless and takes its colour, if it is a dark rum, from the addition of sugar caramel. Some rums are aged like Cognac or Armagnac to gain colour naturally from the cask. The most famous rums come from the West Indies, of which the best known is Jamaica rum. Rum from Martinique, Barbados and Cuba (lighter and drier) are well known.

Schnapps The generic term for strong, dry, usually white spirit in Germany, Holland and Scandinavia.

Slivovitz White plum brandy from Yugoslavia.

Sloe Gin A rather bitter cordial made from sloes macerated in gin.

Strega An Italian sweet liqueur.

Tequila Usually colourless spirit from the fermented juice of the Mexican century plant.

Tia Maria West Indian coffee-flavoured liqueur based on rum.

Vermouth A beverage based on fortified wine and an infusion of herbs. Variations are numerous: French vermouth is pale and relatively dry; Italian vermouth is

dark and sweet. Well-known brand names are Noilly-Prat, Martini-Rossi and Cinzano.

Vodka A clear, tasteless spirit distilled from grain. Popular eastern European vodkas may be flavoured with herbs or berries.

Whiskey *(American)* A spirit distilled from grain which is rather richer and sweeter than Scotch whisky. Bourbon whiskey, from a minimum of 51% corn, comes from Kentucky and Tennessee; rye whiskey will contain at least 51% rye. If these two are blended, they are known as blended whiskey.

Whiskey *(Irish)* A spirit distilled in Ireland from grain, mostly barley; at its best after at least five years' ageing.

Whisky *(Canadian)* A spirit distilled in Canada from cereal grain, generally lighter than American whiskey.

Whisky *(Japanese)* Variations on every sort of Scotch whisky, generally of high quality.

Whisky *(Scotch)* A spirit distilled from grain, unless it is distilled from malted barley, in which case it is known as malt whisky – this is the most famous whisky in the world, and the object of many imitations.

ALCOHOL-FREE MIXED DRINKS

Here are a few ideas for drinks that will not leave drivers or other guests avoiding alcohol feeling ignored. Although still or sparkling mineral water is the best alternative to wine during the meal, the following are suitable for drinks' parties, aperitifs or cocktail gatherings.

Bitters Fizz Add a good dash of bitters to sparkling mineral water. Serve with a slice of lemon and ice.

Fruit Spritzer Pour fruit juice into a tall glass to quarter-fill it, then add sparkling mineral water, ice and lemon or lime slices.

Apple Refresher Make a fruit spritzer with unsweetened apple juice, adding a couple of mint sprigs and a good dash of lemon juice to each glass.

Cola Mixer Half-fill a glass with cola and top it up with tonic water. Add slice of orange and ice.

Grenadine Reviver Pour a little grenadine into a tumbler and add a good dash of lime juice. Top up with sparkling mineral water and add a couple of slices of lime and ice. A sprig of mint may also be added.

Index

A WARD LOCK BOOK

First published in 1996 by Ward Lock, Wellington House, 125 Strand, London WC2R OBB

A Cassell Imprint

Copyright © Ward Lock 1996

Mrs Beeton's is a registered trademark of Ward Lock Ltd

All rights reserved. No part of this book may be reproduced or transmitted in any form or by any means, electronic or mechanical, including photocopying, recording or any information storage and retrieval system, without prior permission in writing from the copyright holder and publisher.

Edited by Jenni Fleetwood
Designed by Jo Tapper

Wine Consultant Steven Spurrier

Photography by Sue Atkinson, Clive Streeter and Andrew Sydenham
Colour artwork by Alison Barratt
Line artwork by Tony Randell

Home Economists Carol Handslip, Jacquie Hine and Lyn Rutherford

British Cataloguing-in-Publication Data
A catalogue record of this book is available from the British Library

ISBN 0-7063-7473-8

Printed and bound in Spain by Bookprint